National 5
Modern Studies

How to Pass

SECOND EDITION

NATIONAL 5

Modern Studies

Frank Cooney, Gary Hughes
and David Sheerin

HODDER
GIBSON
AN HACHETTE UK COMPANY

The Publishers would like to thank the following for permission to reproduce copyright material.

Photo credits p.12 © David Cheskin/WPA Pool/Getty Images; **p.16** (left to right) © The Scottish National Party, © The Scottish Labour Party, © The Scottish Conservative Party, © The Scottish Liberal Democrats Party; **p.23** © Joe Giddens/WPA Pool/Getty Images Europe/ Getty Images; **p.27** (left to right) © The Conservative Party, © The Labour Party, © The Liberal Democrats Party; **p.37** © Ken McKay/ITV via Getty Images; **p.58** © Children's Hearings Scotland; **p.61** © Auremar/stock.adobe.com; **p.62** © Malorny/Moment/Getty Images; **p.71** © Mark Wilson/Getty Images North America/Getty Images; **p.84** © STRINGER/AFP/Getty Images; **p.85** (top to bottom) © The African National Congress Party, © The Democratic Alliance Party, © The Inkatha Freedom Party, Economic Freedom Fighters (EFF) logo; **p.86** © GIANLUIGI GUERCIA/AFP/Getty Images; **p.97** © Mikhail Svetlov/Getty Images Europe/Getty Images; **p.99** © ROPI/Alamy Stock Photo; **p.111** © Mike Goldwater/Alamy Stock Photo; **p.116** © Oxfam; **p.123** © Sipa USA/REX/Shutterstock; **p.125** (top to bottom) © Lt. Col. Leslie Pratt/US Air Force/The Image Works/TopFoto.co.uk, © Image Asset Management Ltd/Alamy; **p.126** (top to bottom) © United Nations, © incamerastock/Alamy Stock Photo; **p.131** (left to right) © Africa Studio/Shutterstock.com, © Artistic Endeavor/ stock.adobe.com

Acknowledgements p.46: Helen McArdle from 'MS Society says many sufferers lost benefits in payment switch', www.heraldscotland.com/news/15507155.Charity_claims_MS_sufferers_are_losing_out_under_benefits_shake_up/?ref=arc (*The Herald*, 1 Sept 2017) reprinted with permission © *The Herald*; **p.53** Data in Figure 7.1 is taken from www.gov.scot/ Resource/0052/00525055.pdf; **pp.58–59** Text under the heading 'The Children's Hearings System', content courtesy of SCRA; **p.60: Michael Matheson, Justice Secretary** from 'The Sunday Herald Holyrood Hustings This week: Law and Order', www. heraldscotland.com/news/homenews/14400571.The_Sunday_Herald_Holyrood_Hustings_This_week__Law_and_Order/ (*The Herald*, 3 April 2016) reprinted with permission © *The Herald*; **p.63** Data in Table 7.2 is taken from www.prisonstudies.org/ world-prison-brief-data

Orders: please contact Bookpoint Ltd, 130 Park Drive, Milton Park, Abingdon, Oxon OX14 4SE. Telephone: (44) 01235 827827. Fax: (44) 01235 400401. Email education@bookpoint.co.uk Lines are open from 9 a.m. to 5 p.m., Monday to Friday, with a 24-hour message answering service. Visit our website at www.hoddereducation.co.uk. If you have queries or questions that aren't about an order, you can contact us at hoddergibson@hodder.co.uk

First published in 2018 by
Hodder Gibson, an imprint of Hodder Education
An Hachette UK Company
211 St Vincent Street
Glasgow, G2 5QY
Impression number 5 4 3

Year 2022 2021 2020

Cover photo © elenabsl / Shutterstock
Illustrations by Aptara, Inc.
Typeset in 13/15 Cronos Pro (Light) by Aptara, Inc.
Printed in Spain
A catalogue record for this title is available from the British Library.
ISBN: 978 1 5104 2102 8

We are an approved supplier on the Scotland Excel framework.

Schools can find us on their procurement system as:
Hodder & Stoughton Limited t/a Hodder Gibson.

MIX
Paper from responsible sources
FSC™ C104740

Contents

Introduction

This revision book will help you to achieve the best possible result in your Modern Studies National 5 examination by explaining clearly what you need to know about the exam and what knowledge and skills you will need to display.

Access to the Hodder Gibson *National 4 & 5 Modern Studies* textbooks will enhance the use of this revision guide.

The textbooks are:

- *Democracy in Scotland and the UK, second edition*
- *Social Issues in the UK, second edition*
- *World Powers and International Issues, second edition.*

You have already covered all or most of the skills and knowledge required to pass National 5, but revision has a very important role to play. By working your way through this book you will find it much easier to understand what you need to display in your assessment answers. This will enhance your confidence and enable you to achieve your full potential.

You will also find advice about the assignment, in which you will have to research a Modern Studies topic or issue of your own choice. This assignment is important as it will be marked by SQA and will contribute to your overall mark and grade.

We hope you will find this book of great value and support.

Good luck!

Part One: How you will be tested

You will have studied the following three Sections:

- Democracy in Scotland and the UK
- Social Issues in the UK
- International Issues.

The National 5 award is made up of two externally marked assessments:

- National 5 question paper (80 marks – 80% of your overall mark)
- National 5 assignment (20 marks – 20% of your overall mark).

Total marks available: 100 marks

The marks you achieve in the question paper and assignment are added together and an overall mark will indicate a pass or fail. From this, your course award will then be graded.

Chapter 1

The exam

The question paper

The question paper is worth a total of 80 marks, with between 26 and 28 marks awarded for each of the three Sections. Across the whole exam paper, there are 30 marks for source-based questions and 50 for knowledge-based questions. Each source-based question will be marked out of 10 marks, and each knowledge and understanding question will be marked out of 4, 6 or 8 marks. You will have 2 hours and 20 minutes to complete the question paper.

What types of questions will I need to answer?

There are three types of skills questions that you will have practised in class and may have answered as part of your unit assessment. These are:

1. Using sources of information to **support and oppose a point of view**. This may have been assessed in your Democracy in Scotland and the UK Section.
2. Using sources of information to **make and justify a decision**. This may have been assessed in your Social Issues in the UK Section.
3. Using sources of information to **draw and support valid conclusions**. This may have been assessed in your International Issues Section.

In Part Five of this book we will look at examples of source-based questions and students' answers.

Remember

In your course exam, the source-based questions can appear in any of the three Sections – so supporting and opposing a point of view could be a question in the International Issues section of the exam.

In the knowledge section of your exam you will answer two types of questions:

1. **Describe** questions, for example:
   Describe, in detail, two ways in which poverty can have a severe impact on families. *4 marks*
2. **Explain** questions, for example:
   Explain, in detail, the disadvantages of the First Past the Post system (FPTP). You should give a maximum of three disadvantages in your answer. *8 marks*

Remember

In your course exam, the knowledge and skills questions for International Issues will not refer to a particular country or a particular issue. You will be expected to base your answer on your knowledge and understanding of your studied World Power or Issue.

Do I have choice?

Your teacher will usually have chosen one topic from each of the three Sections for you to study and you will answer questions on these topics in your exam. Your teacher will have chosen from the following options for each Section:

Section of the course	Option one	Option two
Democracy in Scotland and the UK	Democracy in Scotland	Democracy in the UK
Social Issues in the UK	Social Inequality	Crime and the Law
International Issues	World Powers	World Issues

Hints & tips

What makes a good knowledge answer?

- ✓ *One that answers the question and provides only information that is **relevant** to the question.*
- ✓ *One that is **detailed** and written in paragraphs with clear development of the points you wish to discuss. Remember that one very developed describe answer can gain 3 marks and one very developed explain answer can gain 4 marks.*
- ✓ *One that is an **appropriate length**. Use the number of marks assigned to each question as a guide to how much you should write. Writing long answers for 4-mark questions may make you run out of time in the exam.*
- ✓ *One that uses **up-to-date** examples to illustrate your understanding of the question being asked.*

What makes a bad knowledge answer?

- ✓ *One that does not answer the question, or tries to change the question being asked. This is sometimes called 'turning a question'.*
- ✓ *One that gives detailed description or explanation that is not relevant to the question.*
- ✓ *One that contains information that is out of date (you should be especially careful of this in the International Issues Section).*
- ✓ *One that simply consists of a list of facts with no development. This can receive a maximum of only 2 marks. You must tailor your answer to the question, and only give information that is relevant to what is being asked.*

Remember

Changes to skills question

The skills you can display are:

- ☞ supporting and opposing a point of view
- ☞ drawing and supporting valid conclusions.

These used to be worth 8 marks and are now worth 10 marks.

You must now draw and support four conclusions – increased from three.

Chapter 2
The assignment

Before your exam in May, you will carry out the 'assignment' as part of your National 5 course assessment. Your teacher will probably plan to complete this during the spring term before you sit the exam.

What is the assignment?

The assignment is your personal research on a Modern Studies topic or issue of your own choice. The information collected should display knowledge and understanding of the topic or issue chosen and should include at least two methods of collecting information, with comment on the effectiveness of the methods used.

You will write up the results of your research under controlled assessment conditions on official SQA pro forma sheets. You will be given 1 hour to do this.

The assignment is very important as it is worth a total of 20 marks. Of these, 14 marks are for skills and 6 marks are for knowledge and understanding.

You are allowed to bring two single-sided sheets of A4 paper (containing your notes) into the exam to refer to during the write-up.

What type of hypothesis or issue should I choose?

With agreement from your teacher, you should choose a topic or issue that you feel is appropriate, for example: *'The voting age in all Scottish and UK elections should be reduced to sixteen'.*

You may choose a **hypothesis** or issue from any of the three course Sections or you may choose a topic that integrates two Sections of the course, for example: *'Health inequalities in Scotland and the USA'.*

Some possible titles could include:

- *Voting age should be reduced to sixteen for all UK elections.*
- *Lifestyle choices are the main cause of health inequalities in Scotland.*
- *Foodbanks are the result of poverty.*
- *The 'not proven' verdict does not deliver justice.*
- *The Educational Maintenance Allowance should be given to all 16+ school students.*
- *Police in the UK should not be armed.*
- *The American Dream is not a reality for many US citizens.*
- *America should abolish the death penalty.*

Key words

Hypothesis: A hypothesis is simply a statement that your personal research will try to prove or disprove. If you are being presented at National 5 and you have decided on your topic/issue, it is good practice to state a hypothesis, which you will revisit in your conclusion. However, you could still receive credit for just stating your aims.

Where do I gather information from?

The information gathered for your research can be broken down into two parts: **primary information** and **secondary information**.

Primary information

Primary information is evidence that you have gathered by yourself and is unique to your personal research. If possible, your personal research should contain at least **two** pieces of information gathered by primary research, as well as information gathered from other sources. The ways in which you gather primary evidence can vary greatly – some examples are below:

- surveys/questionnaires
- interviews
- emails
- letters
- focus groups
- field study.

Secondary information

Secondary information is evidence that you have gathered from research that was carried out by others. You should use it to help support your personal research. There is a vast amount of secondary information available, in many different formats – below are just a few examples:

- school textbooks, newspapers and magazines
- internet search engines and websites
- TV and radio programmes
- mobile phone apps
- social media such as Twitter
- library books and articles.

You are expected to evaluate the strengths and weaknesses of each research method you use and to analyse your findings. Remember that **two** methods is the minimum you are required to use and you might wish to widen your range to more than two.

Remember

For the write-up of your research you will need to refer to only two of your research methods. You can include your findings in your notes that you bring in to the exam, as you must refer to these findings in your write-up.

How do I plan my research?

In order to carry out a successful piece of personal research you need to plan it effectively. You will need to keep all evidence of your planning so that your work can be accurately marked.

You may wish to consider the following questions about your primary and secondary sources:

- What useful information have I got from each source to help me research my issue?
- How reliable is the information gathered from each source?
- Could the sources contain bias or exaggeration?

What is a 'pro forma' assignment sheet?

As part of the assignment, you need to demonstrate your understanding, analysis and evaluation of the information you have collected. A self-assessment 'pro forma' sheet is used to do this. The pro forma sheet consists of four sections for you to fill in, with marks allocated to three of the sections. Below is an outline of the sections.

1 Research topic/issue (0 marks)

Your topic should be relevant to Modern Studies and you may discuss your choice with your teacher. The best practice is to present the research question in the form of a hypothesis with clear aims. Do not choose a vague and unfocused topic such as '*A study of poverty in Scotland*'; a better title would be '*The 2013 "bedroom tax" is a tax on the disabled*'. This is written in the form of a hypothesis and allows you to consider to what extent the statement is correct and to consider the evidence that supports and disagrees with the hypothesis. There are no marks for this section but it is good practice to write your title and aims as this will assist you in writing out your research findings and research conclusions.

2 Research methods: collecting relevant evidence from at least two sources (10 marks)

You are expected to evaluate the strengths and weaknesses of the two research methods you have used. You should explain why each method is relevant and highlight its strengths and/or weaknesses. You should make reference to the information that you will take into the assignment.

3 Research findings: presenting your findings clearly (6 marks)

You will have a full page to detail and explain the evidence you have gathered. You may wish to write more and may request extra sheets. The evidence should be balanced and factually correct and you should consider various viewpoints. You should make reference to your A4 information sheet (the notes you bring into the assignment write-up) in your presentation of your findings. Your A4 information sheet should include evidence of primary and/or secondary research and may include, for example, survey results, interview findings, notes from a textbook, newspapers or websites.

4 Research conclusion (4 marks)

Your conclusion should be based on the quality of the research evidence you have presented and should link back to your original hypothesis and aims. Try to avoid just repeating findings already given. At this stage you can indicate what your final thoughts on your issue are.

Remember

Try to base your assignment around a hypothesis rather than just a general study of an issue.

Hints & tips

- ✓ *Research methods section – give as many advantages and disadvantages as possible **but** keep it personal to the research, for example the advantages of a BBC article used. Again, suggest what you would do differently next time for each method.*
- ✓ *Research findings section – there are no marks for copying from your information sheet. You should add relevant knowledge from memory.*
- ✓ *Conclusion section – frame your answer aim by aim with relevant conclusions for each and then come to an overall conclusion.*

Part Two: Democracy in Scotland and the UK

This section of the book provides summary course notes for the Democracy in Scotland and the UK Section of the course.

In the knowledge section of the exam you will answer **three questions** on this Section and these questions will be marked out of 4, 6 or 8 marks each.

What you should know

To be successful in this section, you should:

- ★ be able to **explain** the relationships between each part of the UK political system, including the Scottish Parliament and the UK Parliament
- ★ be **aware** of some of the main issues in the UK political system, including the referendum on Scottish independence.

Introduction to democracy

In a democracy, citizens can participate freely through voting to elect their political representatives. They also have the right to free speech, to join pressure groups and trade unions, and to criticise the government.

Rights and responsibilities

A right is something a person is entitled to; responsibilities are things that people should do or are expected to do. Table 3.1 summarises our rights and responsibilities as citizens of the United Kingdom.

Rights	Responsibilities
To elect our representatives and vote on political issues.	To accept the decision of the majority, even if we disagree.
Those eighteen years old and over can vote in elections.	To be responsible citizens and use our vote in an attempt to influence our representatives.
To express our views in print, on social network sites and in newspapers.	To avoid telling lies or slandering individuals, since this is illegal.
To protest and try to change government legislation such as student tuition fees.	To protest within the law and respect the rights of others.

Table 3.1 Rights and responsibilities

The UK political system

The UK is a parliamentary democracy with a constitutional monarch. This means that the Queen is the ceremonial head of state to the peoples of England, Scotland, Northern Ireland and Wales, but not the head of government.

Figure 3.1 illustrates Scotland's place in the UK political system. The traditional **prerogative powers** of the monarch are held by the UK prime minister and the cabinet. The UK is a unitary system where all powers are vested in the UK Parliament. In this way, the monarch's role in the UK is mostly ceremonial. The UK Government is directly accountable to Parliament.

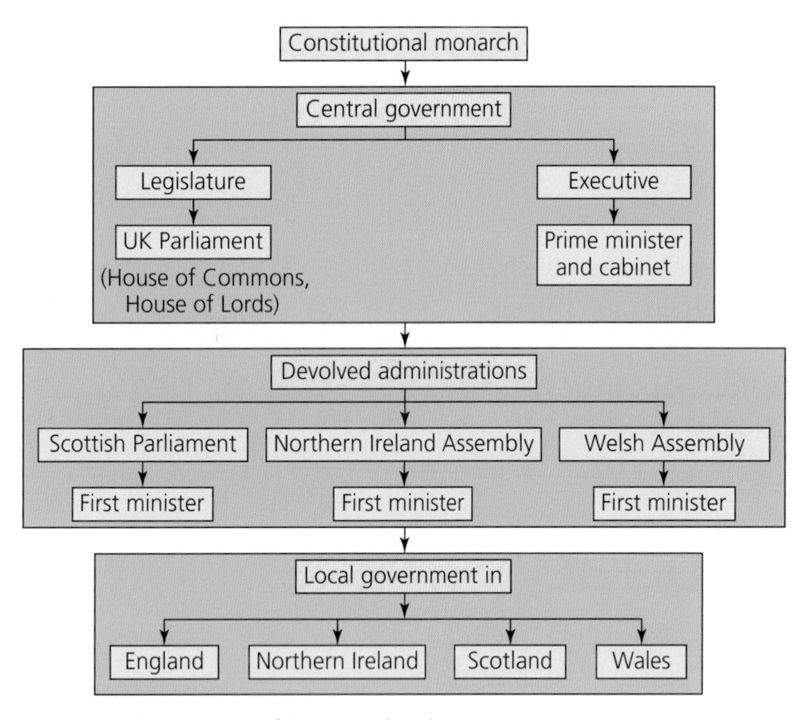

Figure 3.1 The structure of the UK political system

Key words

Prerogative powers: Powers of the monarch that are exercised in the crown's name by the prime minister and government ministers.

Direct democracy: A political system where all citizens vote on every decision taken by the government. The system of democracy used in Ancient Greece.

Referendum: A type of vote where the electorate votes either yes or no on a single political question or issue.

How are decisions made in the UK?

There are two types of democracy: **direct democracy** and representative democracy. The UK has a total population of 60 million, of which Scotland has around 5.2 million. Direct democracy would be impractical here because of the number of citizens. Instead, the UK is a representative democracy. However, the Government can, on occasion, ask the people to vote on a particular issue. This is called a **referendum**. In 2014, the people of Scotland took part in a referendum on Scottish independence and in 2016 the whole of the UK took part in a referendum on membership of the EU.

Representative democracy

The UK is a representative democracy. This means that UK citizens can vote in elections for the people they want to represent their views. These representatives then take decisions on behalf of the people. If voters do not like the decisions their representatives make on their behalf, they can vote for a different representative, called a candidate, at the next election.

Who makes decisions for us?

MP (Member of Parliament)	MSP (Member of Scottish Parliament)
MEP (Member of European Parliament)	Local councillor

	Local council elections	Scottish Parliament elections	UK Parliament elections	European Parliament elections
Frequency of elections	Every four years	Every four years	(At least) every five years	Every five years
Number of representatives	1200 local councillors	129 MSPs	650 MPs	6 MEPs (out of 736)
Responsibilities of representatives	Local services, such as education, housing, roads and refuse collection	Devolved powers, such as health, social work, planning, the environment (see table below)	Reserved powers, such as the economy, immigration, foreign affairs, defence (see table below)	Economic and social affairs, such as setting fishing quotas

Table 3.2 Who makes decisions for us?

Devolved powers	Reserved powers
Health	Defence
Education and training	Social security
Social work	Foreign affairs
Housing	Constitutional matters
Local government	Immigration
Tourism and economic development	Broadcasting
Law and home affairs	Trade and industry
Agriculture, forestry and fishing	Energy: nuclear, coal and gas
Planning	Employment legislation
Police and fire services	Equal opportunities
The environment	Fiscal and monetary system
Sports and the arts	Gambling and the National Lottery
Scottish road network and harbours	Data protection

Table 3.3 Devolved and reserved powers in 1999

Devolution

The Scottish Parliament was established in1999 after the people of Scotland voted in favour of **devolution** in a referendum.

In September 2014, the SNP Government held a referendum to ask the Scottish people the following question:

Should Scotland be an independent country? Yes / No

While the SNP and the Green Party campaigned **FOR** independence, Labour, Conservative and the Liberal Democrats campaigned **AGAINST** independence. The result saw 55% of people voting **NO**. This referendum also saw the passing of legislation in the Scottish Parliament which means that sixteen and seventeen year olds are allowed to vote in referendums and elections held in Scotland.

Key words

Devolution: The transfer of powers from a central body to regional administrations.

Chapter 3
Democracy in Scotland

What you should know

To be successful in this section, you should:

- ★ **understand** the role of an MSP, both in their constituencies and in Parliament
- ★ **know** about the role of the Scottish Parliament, including the functions of the chamber and committees
- ★ have a good **knowledge** about participation and representation in Scotland:
  - ★ have a working **knowledge** of political parties in Scotland and their main policies
  - ★ **understand** the purpose of an election campaign and its main features
  - ★ **understand** the advantages and disadvantages of the Proportional Representation systems used in Scotland – the Additional Member System in the Scottish Parliament.

Hints & tips

In your exam you should try to include examples whenever possible. Go to www.theyworkforyou.com and find out who your MSPs are. You can use them as an example of MSPs.

Representation

Everyone in Scotland has a constituency MSP and seven regional MSPs elected to the Scottish Parliament. Scotland is divided into two groups of geographical areas, called constituencies and regions. There are 73 constituencies, each with its own constituency MSP. These constituencies lie within eight regions and each region has seven 'list' MSPs, giving a total of 56 regional MSPs. This gives a total of 129 MSPs within the Scottish Parliament.

Hints & tips

Visit www.parliament.scot/msps/constituency-maps.aspx to see a map of the eight regions and constituency maps for each region.

The role of an MSP

An MSP's working life is divided into two distinct roles: work within their constituency/region; and work within the Scottish Parliament.

Hints & tips

An exam question could be based on the work carried out within an MSP's constituency or region, or the work they carry out at Parliament.

Parliamentary work	Constituency work
Debating: Every MSP will participate in some debates. This gives MSPs the chance to put forward the views of their constituents. For example, if there are plans to reduce the number of nurses in the NHS within Scotland, this may directly affect some constituencies with hospitals, e.g. Edinburgh Royal Infirmary.	**Surgeries:** Usually scheduled once a week, an MSP will visit various areas within their constituency or region for an open advice clinic, known as a surgery. Constituents can drop in to the surgery to express concerns that they have directly to their MSP. These concerns could be about local issues as well as national issues.
Voting on new laws: Every MSP has to vote on whether they agree or disagree with each proposed new law, known as a Bill. For example, they could vote for or against a proposal to lower the voting age to sixteen.	**Attending meetings:** MSPs will attend a huge number of meetings when they are in their constituencies. For example, he or she may meet local charities to listen to their views on current government policy.
Question time (FMQT): Every government department will have a 'question time' within Parliament where MSPs get the chance to question the Government directly. At First Minister's Question Time (FMQT), an MSP could have the chance to challenge the FM directly about government decisions and express his or her constituents' concerns.	**Local media:** In order to keep a good profile within their constituency or region MSPs will often appear in local newspapers or on local TV and radio. Quite often MSPs will raise awareness of local issues or highlight local charities using the media and communicate their thoughts about these.
Committee work: MSPs can become members of a committee. This gives them an opportunity to look at a specific issue in depth. An example of this is if an MSP is interested in educational issues they could sit on the Education and Culture Committee, perhaps looking at the impact of a Curriculum for Excellence.	**Visits and social events:** An MSP is often regarded as a high profile guest for many different organisations and as a result MSPs will spend a large proportion of their time attending various events, for example the opening of a new business or a school's awards ceremony.
Written answers: An MSP can submit a written question to the Government and receive a reply. He or she could then relay this to a concerned constituent.	**Local party meetings:** MSPs will meet occasionally with local party members to discuss issues that concern the party as a whole. The MSP will then relay this information to the party's leadership.
Members' Bills: MSPs also have the chance to submit their own ideas for new laws. Every year they can submit up to two of their own Bills. If they pass through Parliament they could become new laws. Margo MacDonald MSP submitted her own Assisted Suicide Bill; however, this has not been successfully passed through the Scottish Parliament.	**Constituent letters, emails and social media:** MSPs receive a large volume of letters and emails from constituents and local groups on local and national issues. In order to manage this, MSPs will have a constituency office and employ a number of staff. Increasingly, MSPs also use social media such as Twitter and Facebook to communicate with constituents and hear their views.

Table 3.4 The role of an MSP

The Scottish Parliament

All the MSPs elected to the Scottish Parliament work within the debating chamber of the Parliament. The governing party sits in the middle of the chamber and the opposition parties sit on either side.

Remember

Unlike the UK Parliament, the Scottish Parliament only has one chamber, called the debating chamber, which is fully elected. The UK Parliament has two chambers. The House of Commons is elected; the House of Lords is an appointed chamber.

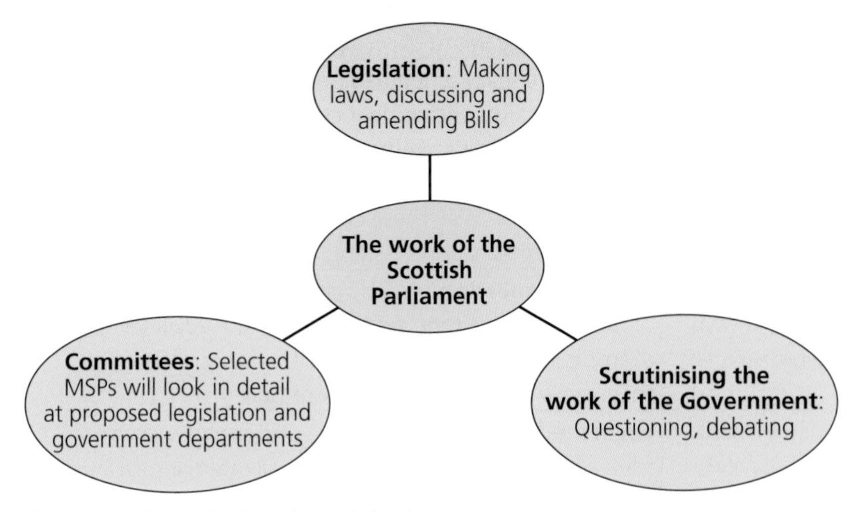

Figure 3.2 The work of the Scottish Parliament

Following the Scotland Act 2016 there will be a number of new powers coming to the Scottish Parliament. New areas such as equal opportunities, abortion law, speed limits and gaming machines as well as tax, welfare, Air Passenger Duty and the licensing of onshore oil and gas extraction are due to be transferred to Holyrood over the next few years.

Roles within the Scottish Parliament

First minister

The first minister is the leader of the governing party. In most cases this will be the party with the most seats in the chamber. Due to the **party whip**, government MSPs usually obey the first minister's wishes. The first minister also has the power to appoint whom he or she wants to the cabinet and this gives him or her **power of patronage**. If a party's MSPs have ambitions to gain a position in the cabinet they would do well to fully support their party leader. The first minister is accountable to the Scottish Parliament.

Figure 3.3 First Minister Nicola Sturgeon

Cabinet

The first minister appoints MSPs from his or her party to run government departments. There is a government department to look after each of the devolved powers listed in Table 3.3. Two of the most powerful positions in the cabinet are the finance secretary, in charge of government finances, and the deputy first minister, who works closely with the first minister in shaping policy.

Leaders of opposition parties

The current leaders of the opposition parties are Richard Leonard (Labour), Ruth Davidson (Conservative) and Willie Rennie (Liberal Democrat). The leaders of the opposition parties are seen as the chief critics of the Government, but they do not have any direct power within the chamber. The opposition parties select MSPs from their own parties to form a shadow cabinet, which scrutinises the policies and decisions of the government departments.

Key words

Party whip: The party whip is appointed by the leadership of a political party to persuade or pressurise MSPs into supporting the party – this is called following the party line.

Power of patronage: The power to appoint or remove individuals from office.

Public petitions

Members of the public can raise a 'national issue' with Parliament by registering a public petition. The Public Petitions Committee will consider what action should be taken. Public petitions have resulted in:

- a ban on smoking in public places
- the restoration of a railway link to the Borders.

Hints & tips

Visit www.scottish.parliament.uk/gettinginvolved/petitions to check out current petitions or even to start one of your own!

How representative is the Scottish Parliament?

Ethnic minorities and women have not been well represented in the Scottish Parliament since it was established in 1999.

There are currently two MSPs from a non-white background – less than 2% of all MSPs. The Scottish ethnic minority population is around 8%.

Women are also not fairly represented in the Scottish Parliament. Only 35% of MSPs are female (45 out of 129 MSPs), although 51% of the Scottish population is female.

Why is female representation in the Scottish Parliament higher than the UK Parliament?

In the UK Parliament, 32% of MPs are female compared with 35% in the Scottish Parliament. The gap between the two Parliaments has narrowed substantially in recent years, however. Reasons for the continued gap include:

- the working hours of the Scottish Parliament are much more family friendly than those of the UK Parliament
- there are modern crèche facilities within the Parliament
- through the regional vote, political parties can promote more female MSPs.

Committees in the Scottish Parliament

Committees in the Scottish Parliament carry out an essential role in scrutinising the Government and play a central part in the passing of laws.

They scrutinise the work of the Scottish Parliament by holding inquiries, examining new and existing legislation and taking evidence from key stakeholders. Some even consider public petitions from individuals and groups who want to see change happen.

As of September 2017 the following committees were in operation:

Committees
Culture, Tourism, Europe and External Relations Committee
Delegated Powers and Law Reform Committee
Economy, Jobs and Fair Work Committee
Edinburgh Bakers' Widows' Fund Bill Committee
Education and Skills Committee
Environment, Climate Change and Land Reform Committee
Equalities and Human Rights Committee
Finance and Constitution Committee
Health and Sport Committee
Justice Committee
Justice Sub-committee on Policing
Local Government and Communities Committee
Pow of Inchaffray Drainage Commission (Scotland) Bill Committee

Public Audit and Post-legislative Scrutiny Committee
Public Petitions Committee
Rural Economy and Connectivity Committee
Social Security Committee
Standards, Procedures and Public Appointments Committee
Writers to the Signet Dependants' Annuity Fund Amendment (Scotland) Bill Committee

Table 3.5 Scottish Parliament committees

There are fifteen committees, most of which have between seven and eleven member MSPs. Each committee also has a convener and a deputy convener who chair the meetings. Membership and convenership have to reflect the balance of political power within the Parliament as a whole. For example, the whole of the Education and Skills Committee could not be made up of only Labour MSPs. This ensures that the work of committees does not become party political.

Committees can be set up by Parliament for long- and short-term purposes. They can also be Mandatory or Select Committees.

Case study: Scrutinising policy – the Rural Economy and Connectivity Committee

About: The Rural Economy and Connectivity Committee meets every Wednesday morning. Its primary role is to scrutinise the policies and performance of the Scottish Government and its agencies in matters related to transport, agriculture and other areas. Edward Mountain, MSP for the Highlands and Islands, is convener of the committee.

Example of work: The Rural Economy and Connectivity Committee scrutinised proposed legislation relating to the use of seat belts on school transport. The Seat Belts on School Transport (Scotland) Bill 2017 was introduced by Gillian Martin MSP and called for a legal requirement that all home-to-school transport have seat belts fitted. In considering this fairly simple and popular bill the committee also suggested the following amendments in addition to Gillian Martin's proposal:

- The committee highlighted several additional issues related to the use of seat belts on school transport, which were not covered by the Bill. The committee suggested that no distinction should be made between travel on dedicated home-to-school transport and that on a school excursion. Therefore, the committee strongly recommended that the Bill's provisions should be extended to cover excursions or trips organised by schools.
- The committee was surprised to discover there is currently no legal requirement for children aged three to fourteen to wear seat belts where they are fitted on buses and coaches. It strongly encouraged the Scottish Government to work closely with the UK Government and other stakeholders to seek an early resolution in this matter.
- The committee considered that a package of guidance and practical support should be provided to supplement the Bill's provisions, covering such issues as behavioural change, monitoring of seat belt use and duty of care.

Case study: Inquiry into the gender pay gap – Economy, Jobs and Fair Work Committee

This committee had the following remit: *To explore the effect of the gender pay gap on the Scottish economy, with a particular focus on business performance, the Scottish public sector and Scottish Government action required to address the issue.*

It published a report on 26 June 2017 called *No Small Change* in which it challenged the Government to do more to reduce the gender pay gap. It made 38 recommendations and observations on which it wanted the Government to act, including changing the way that the Government records the gender pay gap, asking that the Government take action to increase the number of females in education who embark on STEM (Science, Technology, Engineering and Maths) careers and concerns that only companies with more than 250 employees need to report their gender pay gaps, as they feel that this may 'hide' the true nature of the pay gap.

During its inquiry the committee heard evidence from many witnesses including Debbie Miller, Inclusion Manager at RBS (Royal Bank of Scotland); Nicky Page, Head of People Management, Police Scotland; and Anna Ritchie Allan from Close the Gap. The committee also made a number of visits to workplaces such as the Wood Group and domestic cleaning agency Home Sweet Home.

Following the report, the Scottish Government made a written response to the committee addressing each of their points. The Minister with responsibility, Jamie Hepburn MSP, reassured the committee of the Government's determination to reduce gender inequality and improve women's position in the workplace and indeed in all aspects of Scottish life.

Political parties in Scotland

There are four main political parties in Scotland: the Scottish National Party, the Scottish Labour Party, the Scottish Conservative Party and the Scottish Liberal Democrat Party. There are also smaller parties such as the Scottish Green Party.

What do political parties do?

Most MSPs and councillors are affiliated with a political party. Once elected, MSPs and councillors connected to a political party are expected to represent the policies of the party.

Before an election, political parties will produce their ideas of how, if elected, they will try to improve the country. These ideas are known as policies. As part of the election campaign, the parties will collate these ideas in their **party manifestos**, which voters and the media can read.

The aim of a political party is to win as many seats as possible in an election. The more seats they win, the greater the influence the party will have in how the country is run and the easier it will be for them to put their policies into action.

Key words

Party manifesto: A party publication which contains the policies they hope to implement, if elected.

Political parties in Scotland and their policies

Political party	Scottish National Party	Scottish Labour	Scottish Conservatives	Scottish Liberal Democrats
	SNP www.snp.org	Scottish Labour	Scottish Conservatives	SCOTTISH LIBERAL DEMOCRATS
Leader in 2017	Nicola Sturgeon	Richard Leonard	Ruth Davidson	Willie Rennie
Key policies	• To lead Scotland to independence. • To maintain free university tuition for students who normally live in Scotland.	• Keep Scotland as part of the UK. • Deliver a public-owned railway system.	• Keep Scotland as part of the UK. • To maintain Scotland's nuclear deterrent.	• To keep Scotland as part of the UK but push for more powers for the Scottish Parliament. • To oppose the construction of more nuclear power plants in Scotland.

Table 3.6 Political parties in Scotland and their key policies

The SNP majority Government

Following the 2011 Scottish Parliament elections, the SNP won the election with a majority. This sent shockwaves through Scottish politics, as the Additional Member System (AMS) was designed to prevent any one party gaining an overall majority. However, the 2016 Scottish election saw the SNP form a **minority** Government with fewer than half the seats. This is despite improved popularity. Many claim this is because AMS ensured a more balanced Parliament.

Elections

How do party volunteers help in election campaigns?

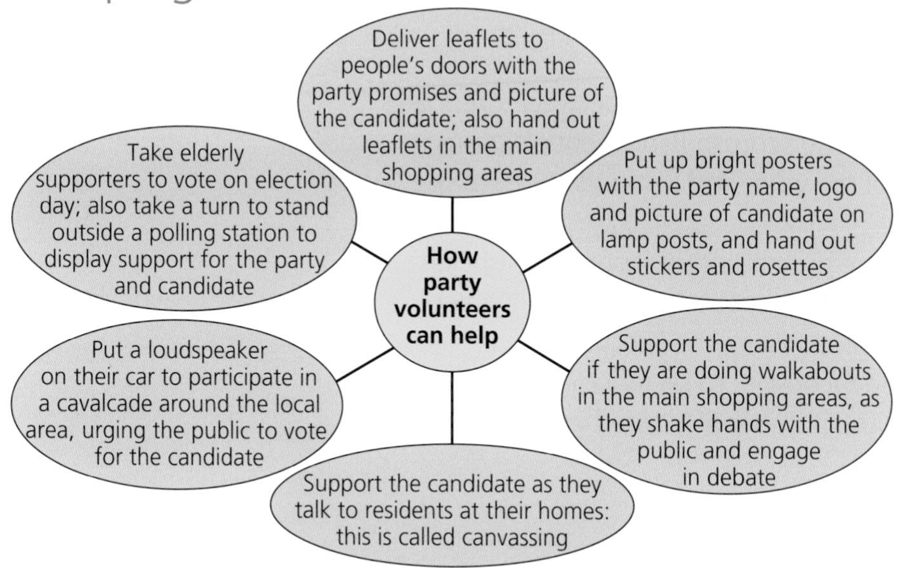

Figure 3.4 Ways in which party volunteers can help in election campaigns

Electoral systems

Proportional Representation

The electoral system used for the Scottish Parliament and Scottish local authority elections is called Proportional Representation (PR). In a PR system, there is a more direct link between the number of votes received and the number of seats won. For the Scottish Parliament elections the PR system used is called the Additional Member System (AMS).

> **Hints & tips**
>
> *You may be asked about the advantages or disadvantages of AMS. It is important that you try to include examples in your answer if you wish to gain full marks.*

Additional Member System

The Scottish Parliament, Welsh Assembly and London Assembly are all elected using the Additional Member System (AMS). The system is a mixture of First Past the Post (FPTP) and PR. In Scotland voters cast two votes.

- The first vote uses FPTP to elect the 73 winning candidates in the local constituency elections.
- The second vote allows voters to choose between parties in a multi-member constituency. The country is divided into eight regional lists and each region elects seven regional list MSPs.

The 56 regional list MSPs are added to the 73 constituency MSPs to give a total of 129 MSPs in the Scottish Parliament.

Until the 2011 Scottish Parliament election no party had won a majority of seats. This led to the creation of Labour and Liberal Democrat **coalition governments** after the 1999 and 2003 elections and a minority SNP government after the 2007 election. Following the 2016 election the SNP formed a minority government.

Key words

Coalition government: When two or more political parties form a government to run the country.

Arguments in favour of AMS

- AMS is 'fair' because it produces a close correlation between the share of votes and the share of seats. In the Scottish Parliament elections in 2016, Labour won about 21% of the votes and just under 20% of the seats.
- PR can give minority parties more parliamentary representation. In the 2003 elections for the Scottish Parliament the AMS system enabled the Scottish Socialist Party, the Green Party, the Scottish Senior Citizens Unity Party and the Independents to be represented.
- It is argued that PR will reduce the number of 'wasted votes' and so encourage greater voter turnout.

Arguments against AMS

- AMS can create a government in which a minority party can implement its policies. The Liberal Democrats finished fourth in the 2003 Scottish election, yet formed a government with Labour.
- It can lead to an unstable and weak government. The minority SNP Government of 2007–11 found it difficult to implement its policies. It failed, for example, to implement its policy of minimum pricing of alcohol in November 2010.
- It breaks the link between constituency and representative. We each have eight MSPs who represent us: one constituency and seven regional. Many people find this confusing.

Hints & tips

In order to try and remember the arguments for and against AMS you could try to make up a mnemonic to aid your learning.

*For example, the arguments **for** could be: **C.L.E.N.***

- ✓ ***Coalition** – more likely to result in coalitions so more people are represented in government.*
- ✓ ***Link** – closer link between percentage of votes and percentage of seats.*
- ✓ ***Encourage** – under AMS there are fewer wasted votes so it is supposed to encourage turnout.*
- ✓ ***Normal** – other countries, such as Germany, use systems similar to AMS.*

See if you can make one up of your own for the arguments against.

Questions and model answers

Describe question

Political parties campaign to get their candidates elected as MSPs in a number of ways.

Describe, **in detail**, **two** ways in which political parties campaign to get their candidates elected as MSPs. **4 marks**

Remember

Knowledge and understanding questions will have 4, 6 or 8 marks allocated and you will need to answer three questions 'describing' or 'explaining.'

Model answer

Political parties campaign to get their candidates elected in a number of different ways. One way is to canvass voters. Parties will employ a number of volunteers who will work alongside the candidates as they go door-to-door or even telephone households. They canvass voters by discussing the election with them in person and in doing so try to gain their vote.

Another way political parties help in election campaigns is by producing a large variety of promotional materials. These may take the form of leaflets that are delivered through the doors of voters and even huge billboard posters in town centres such as Falkirk to promote their candidates for Scottish Parliament elections. For example, in many constituencies during elections, lamp posts are usually covered in placards with a candidate's name on them and quite often cars drive around the streets with loudspeakers through which a message is played to support a campaign.

Marker's comments

This is a very good answer because it is both relevant and detailed. Each point is fully explained, with examples from Scottish Parliament elections where possible. Each paragraph clearly includes at least one point that addresses the question and the candidate is showing clearly that they understand the question completely. This answer would gain full marks. **4 marks**

Hints & tips

- ✓ *For 4 or 6 marks, you must describe **two** ways in which political parties campaign.*
- ✓ *Include examples when you can and make sure you fully explain your points.*
- ✓ *Try to write as much detail as you can in the time given; there are no prizes for finishing first!*

Explain question

The Additional Member System (AMS) is used to elect MSPs to the Scottish Parliament. There are advantages and disadvantages to the system.

Explain, **in detail**, three advantages and/or disadvantages of AMS. **8 marks**

Model answer

The AMS voting system has been used in the Scottish Parliament election system since 1999. One advantage of AMS is that it is a Proportional Representation system so there will be a closer link between the share of votes and the share of the seats. For example, in the 2011 Scottish Parliament election the Scottish Conservatives gained 13% of the votes and 12% of the seats. This is seen by many as being 'fairer' to the voters, as the number of MSPs will reflect each party's popularity.

However, having two MSPs creates a disadvantage as it creates a two-tier system of MSPs. Constituency MSPs, such as Nicola Sturgeon, have been directly elected by their constituency residents and so there will be a strong link between the representative and the people in the constituency. However, the people of Glasgow Southside who voted for Nicola Sturgeon also have seven regional MSPs that have been chosen by the political parties. It is thought that the link between constituents and this type of MSP is not so strong.

Another disadvantage of AMS is that it usually results in a coalition government. A Labour–Liberal Democrat coalition government led the Scottish Parliament between 1999 and 2007. Many people see this as a disadvantage because the Government's policies have to be renegotiated after the election and so the original manifesto promises are sometimes not carried out. Another criticism is that AMS can give a political party more power than it is entitled to based on the number of votes it received. For example, in 2016 the Scottish Greens, in return for enabling the SNP minority Government to pass its budget, 'persuaded' the SNP to change its budget plans. The SNP decided not to increase the threshold for paying 40% tax in Scotland, yet the Greens had received only 6% of the votes in the 2016 Scottish Parliament elections.

Marker's comments

This answer is a brilliant example as it clearly addresses the question. It looks at four separate arguments and provides excellent and up-to-date examples to help enhance the response. The candidate shows his or her deeper knowledge by including examples of current politicians and election results. The answer also provides both advantages and disadvantages, giving it balance. Due to the detail and exemplification, each of the paragraphs is worth 4 marks. As the maximum number of marks available is 8, the answer would be awarded 8/8.

8 marks

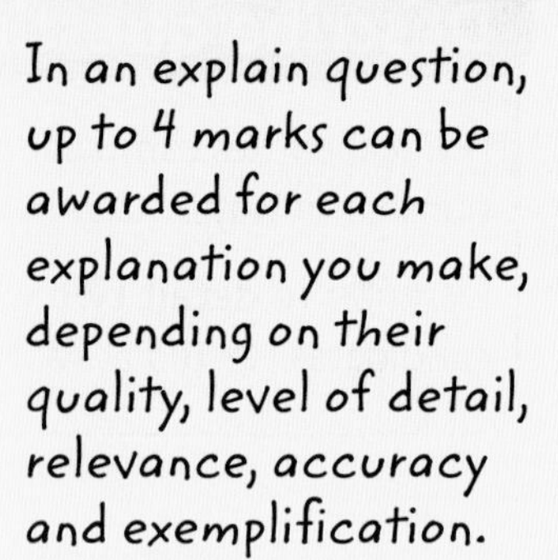

Remember

In an explain question, up to 4 marks can be awarded for each explanation you make, depending on their quality, level of detail, relevance, accuracy and exemplification.

Hints & tips

- ✓ *For 8 marks, you must come up with* ***three*** *separate arguments for you answer.*
- ✓ *For each point, ensure you use exemplification to enhance your answer.*
- ✓ *Try to write as much detail as you can in the time given; there are no prizes for finishing first!*

Chapter 4

Democracy in the UK

What you should know

To be successful in this section, you should:

★ **understand** the role of an MP, both in their constituencies and in Parliament

★ **know** about the role of the UK Parliament, including the functions of the House of Commons and the House of Lords

★ have a good **knowledge** about participation and representation in the UK:

  - ★ have a working **knowledge** of political parties in the UK and be able to describe the main policies of the main parties: the Conservatives, Labour and the Liberal Democrats
  - ★ **understand** the purpose of an election campaign and its main features
  - ★ **understand** the advantages and disadvantages of the First Past the Post electoral system and understand the importance of elections for democracy in the UK.

Representation

What is an MP?

Everyone in the UK has a Member of Parliament (MP) who represents them within the UK Parliament. The UK is divided into 650 geographical areas called constituencies and every constituency has its own MP. There are 533 constituencies in England, 59 in Scotland, 40 in Wales and 18 in Northern Ireland.

The role of an MP

An MP's working life is divided into two distinct roles: work within their constituency and work within the UK Parliament.

Hints & tips

In your exam you should try to include examples whenever possible. Go to http://findyourmp.parliament.uk and find out who your MP is. You can use them as an example of an MP in your work.

Hints & tips

An exam question could be based on the work carried out within an MP's constituency and/or the work they carry out at Parliament.

Parliamentary work	Constituency work
Debating: Every MP will participate in some debates. This gives MPs the chance to put forward the views of their constituents. For example, if there are plans to reduce the number of soldiers in the armed forces, this may directly affect some constituencies with army bases, e.g. Leuchars Airbase near St Andrews.	**Surgeries:** Usually scheduled once a week, an MP will visit various areas within his or her constituency for an open advice clinic known as a surgery. Constituents can drop in to the surgery to express concerns that they have directly to their MP. These concerns could be about local issues as well as national issues.
Voting on new laws: Every MP has to vote on whether they agree or disagree with a proposed new law, known as a Bill. For example, they could vote for or against a proposal to lower the voting age to sixteen for UK elections.	**Attending meetings:** MPs will attend a huge number of meetings when they are in their constituencies. For example, they may meet with local charities to listen to their views on current government policy.
Question time (PMQs): Every government department will have a question time within Parliament where MPs get the chance to question the Government directly, including the prime minister. At Prime Minister's Questions (PMQs) an MP could have the chance to challenge the PM directly about government decisions and express his or her constituents' concerns.	**Local media:** In order to keep a good profile within their constituencies MPs will often appear in local newspapers or on local TV and radio. Quite often MPs will raise awareness of local issues or highlight local charities using the media and communicate their thoughts about these.
Committee work: MPs can become members of a select committee. This gives them an opportunity to look at a specific issue in depth. An example of this is if an MP is interested in the UK's exit from the European Union they could sit on the Constitution Committee and scrutinise the Government's plans.	**Visits and social events:** An MP is often regarded as a high profile guest for many different organisations and as a result MPs will spend a large proportion of their time attending various events, for example the opening of a new business or a school's awards ceremony.
Written answers: An MP can submit a written question to the Government and receive a reply. He or she could then relay this to a concerned constituent.	**Local party meetings:** MPs will meet occasionally with local party members to discuss issues that concern the party as a whole. The MP will then feedback this information to the party's leadership.
Private Members' Bills (PMB): MPs also have the chance to submit their own ideas for new laws. Every year a small number are selected and if they pass through Parliament they could become new laws. Perhaps the most well known PMB is the Murder Act 1965, which abolished the death penalty within the UK.	**Constituent letters, emails and social media:** MPs receive a large volume of letters and emails from constituents and local groups on local and national issues. In order to manage this, MPs will have a constituency office and employ a number of staff. Increasingly, MPs also use social media such as Twitter and Facebook to communicate with constituents and hear their views.

Table 4.1 The role of an MP

The UK Parliament

Monarch	The monarch is the reigning head of state. Queen Elizabeth II has been the monarch of the UK since 1952.
House of Lords	This is the upper house in Parliament and is mainly an advisory chamber. It is made up from peers, some of whom have been appointed due to their expertise in a particular subject and others who are life peers.
House of Commons	This is the lower house and dominant chamber of Parliament. It consists of Members of Parliament (MPs) who have been elected by the UK public. Its two key roles are legislation and scrutiny of government.

Table 4.2 The UK Parliament

The House of Commons

All of the MPs elected in the general election work within the House of Commons. The House of Commons operates on the principle of debate and therefore is an **adversarial system**. Members of the governing party sit on one side of the chamber and the opposition parties sit on the other side.

Legislation	All MPs are involved in making laws and discussing and amending Bills.
Committees	Selected MPs will be on committees that look in detail at proposed legislation and government departments.
Scrutinising the work of the Government	All MPs question the work of the Government and debate relevant issues.

Table 4.3 The work of the House of Commons

Key words

Adversarial system: A relationship in which two or more organisations oppose each other.

Party whip: The party whip is appointed by the leadership of a political party to persuade or pressurise MPs into supporting the party – this is called following the party line.

Power of patronage: The power to appoint or remove individuals from office.

Roles within the UK Parliament

Prime minister

The prime minister is the leader of the governing party. As in the Scottish Parliament, in most cases this will be the party with the most seats in the House of Commons. **Party whips** perform the same role in the UK Parliament as they do in the Scottish Parliament and government MPs usually obey the prime minister's wishes. The prime minister appoints whom she or he wants to the cabinet (**power of patronage**) and it is in the interests of MPs to support their party leader if they want to be given a role in the cabinet. Like the first minister in Scotland, the prime minister is the public face of the Government.

Figure 4.1 Prime Minister Theresa May

The prime minister appoints MPs and peers from his or her party to run government departments. There is a government department to look after each of the devolved and reserved powers listed in Table 3.3. Two of the most powerful positions in the UK cabinet are the chancellor of the exchequer, who is in charge of government finances and taxation, and the foreign secretary.

Remember

Cabinet ministers are not responsible for devolved powers. For instance, education and health ministers are only in charge of education and health services in England.

Party	Number of seats	Percentage of seats
Conservatives	318	48.9
Labour	262	40.3
Liberal Democrats	12	1.8
Democratic Unionist Party (DUP)	10	1.5
Others (including SNP)	48	7.4

Table 4.4 2017 general election results

Leader of the opposition

This is a high profile position and the leader of the opposition receives a lot of media attention. They are seen as the chief critic of the Government and although they do not have any direct power within the House of Commons, they can have a big influence in the popularity of the Government. The opposition party selects its own MPs to form a shadow cabinet, which scrutinises the policies and decisions of the Government.

> **Hints & tips**
>
> *Make sure you know at least two or three members of the UK Government. Visit www.gov.uk/government/ministers*

How representative is the House of Commons?

Ethnic minorities and women are not well represented in the UK Parliament.

The UK ethnic minority population is around 16% but the results from the 2017 general election show that only around 8% of MPs are from a non-white background.

Similarly, 32% of MPs are female (208 out of 650), whereas 51% of the UK population is female.

Reasons for the poor representation of ethnic minorities and women are thought to include:

- the working hours of the UK Parliament often result in women with families being put off becoming MPs
- there is a white male culture within the House of Commons
- political parties do not select enough women and ethnic minority candidates for elections.

> **Hints & tips**
>
> *Make sure you study the work of an MP in Parliament as this will also enhance your knowledge of the House of Commons (see page 23).*

The House of Lords

The House of Lords, also known as the Second Chamber or Upper House, is an appointed chamber – members are not elected by the public. They play an advisory role in Parliament – they are not involved in running the country on a day-to-day basis but they can still have a lot of influence in the law-making process. The people who sit in the House of Lords are called peers and they have the title Lord or Baroness.

Legislation	All Bills are debated in the House of Lords before they become law.
Committees	Some peers are appointed because they have experience in a specific area. They then sit on committees that look into relevant matters.
Scrutinising the work of the Government	Government matters are questioned and debated in the House of Lords.

Table 4.5 The work of the House of Lords

How does the Lords affect decision-making?

Many people believe the House of Lords to be an important part of the UK Parliament for the following reasons:

- Through the work of committees they can amend Bills passing through Parliament.
- Many Lords are experts in a particular field and can offer sound advice on new legislation.
- The Lords can potentially delay non-financial Bills by up to one year.
- By disagreeing with the Government they may be able to force a rethink on policy.

How are Lords appointed?

The vast majority of members of the House of Lords are life peers – people who have been selected by governments (over the years) due to their expertise in specific fields. In contrast, hereditary peers are people who have inherited a title from someone in their family. The number of hereditary peers was reduced substantially after reforms in 1999 and the current hereditary peers are now unable to pass on their titles. There are also a small number of Lords spiritual, who are bishops from the Church of England.

Once a Lord accepts his or her place in the House of Lords the appointment is for the rest of their life (but cannot be passed on to their descendants).

Issues with the House of Lords

A common theme within recent politics has been reform of the House of Lords. Many people feel that as the House of Lords is an unelected chamber it is not democratic. Many governments have tried to reform the role of the chamber.

House of Lords Act 1999

This Act reduced the number of hereditary peers in the House of Lords to 92 and by July 2012 there were only 89 hereditary peers. Since 1999 many governments have tried to reform the House of Lords further but largely without success. However, in 2009 the UK Court of Appeal – the highest appeal court in the UK – was moved from the House of Lords to the UK Supreme Court.

House of Lords Reform Bill 2012

In 2012, the coalition Government recommended that the number of peers be reduced from 826 to 450 and that 80% of members should be elected rather than appointed. They also recommended that the number of Church of England bishops be reduced and that a time limit on the term to be served be introduced. Peers would no longer be members for life but would serve a non-renewable fifteen-year term instead. The Bill did not make it through Parliament because there was not enough support from backbench Conservative MPs.

Differences between the House of Commons and the House of Lords

House of Commons	House of Lords
Elected MPs.	Appointed peers.
MPs can be from any background and have any qualifications.	Most peers are appointed due to their expertise in a specific field.
MPs have to win an election every five years.	Once appointed, Lords and Baronesses have the position for life.
MPs are paid a salary plus expenses.	Peers receive only an allowance and expenses.
MPs represent constituents.	Peers represent only themselves.
Nearly all MPs are members of a political party.	Many peers are members of a political party but a large number are not.

Table 4.6 Differences between the two Houses of Parliament

Participation

There are three main political parties in the UK: the Conservatives, Labour and the Liberal Democrats. There are also smaller parties including the Green Party and the UK Independence Party.

What do political parties do?

Most MPs and Lords within the UK Parliament are affiliated with political parties. Once elected, MPs connected to a political party are expected to represent the policies of the party. If an MP does not do this they can be removed from the party and will not have the party's support at the next general election.

Before an election, political parties will create their own ideas of how, if elected, they will try to improve the country. These ideas are known as policies. As part of the election campaign, the parties will collate these ideas in their **party manifestos**, which voters and the media can read.

The aim of a political party is to win as many seats as possible in an election. The more seats they win, the greater the influence the party will have in how the country is run and the easier it will be for them to put their policies into action.

Key words

Party manifesto: A party publication which contains the policies they hope to implement, if elected.

Political parties in the UK and their policies

Political party	Conservatives	Labour	Liberal Democrats
Leader in 2017	Theresa May Conservatives	Jeremy Corbyn Labour	Sir Vince Cable LIBERAL DEMOCRATS
Key policies	• To get the best Brexit deal. • To make the economy work for everyone. • To tackle the injustices that hold people back.	• To nationalise the railways into public ownership. • To scrap student tuition fees in England and Wales. • To increase free childcare provisions.	• To have a second referendum on leaving the EU. • To end imprisonment for possession of illegal drugs for personal use. • To ban the sale of diesel cars by 2025.

Table 4.7 Political parties in the UK and their policies

Hung parliament

The Conservative Government lost its majority in the House of Commons after the election in 2017 and so, as no one party had a majority, it became a hung parliament. The Government was forced to make an agreement with the Democratic Unionist Party (DUP) of Northern Ireland to enable them to drive through their policies in Parliament. Without a majority, governments are more likely to be embarrassed by being overruled by opposition parties and this can lead to instability.

Elections

What role do political parties play in election campaigns?

Political parties co-ordinate election campaigns in the weeks and months before a general election or a by-election (held when an MP retires, resigns or dies in the period between general elections).

Political parties invest large amounts of money trying to get their candidates elected. Some of this money is spent on designing and printing posters and leaflets to help promote a candidate.

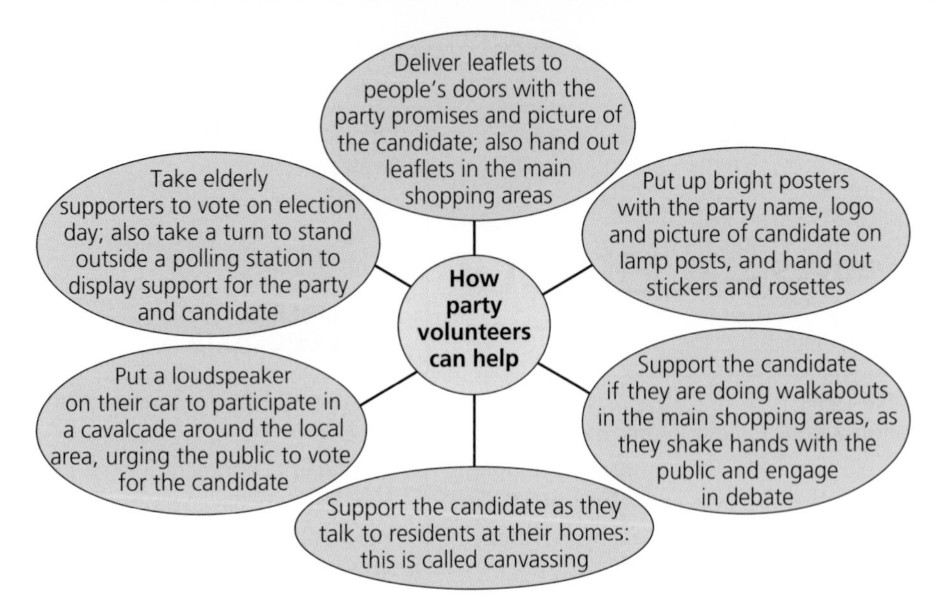

Figure 4.2 Ways in which party volunteers can help in election campaigns

Electoral system

First Past the Post

In a general election, each of the 650 constituencies in the UK elects one Member of Parliament (MP).The candidate who wins the most votes in a constituency becomes the MP. The electoral system used to elect members to the UK Parliament is called First Past the Post (FPTP). This is a simple majority system – sometimes called the winner-takes-all system.

Advantages of FPTP

- It usually provides a strong single-party government and allows the prime minister and the cabinet to pursue policies clearly stated in their election manifesto.
- The system prevents extremist parties from obtaining representation. The British National Party (BNP) achieved over half a million votes in the 2010 general election but gained no seats.
- It is easy to understand and implement. Voters vote only once and the results are announced very quickly. In contrast there were 140,000 spoilt ballot papers in the 2007 Scottish Parliament elections, which was under a different electoral system.

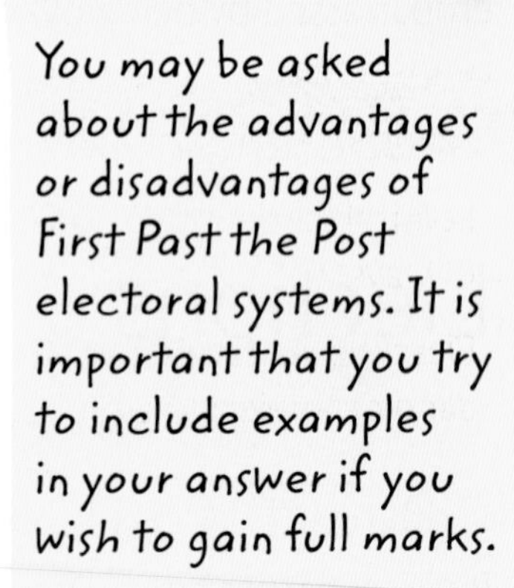

Disadvantages of FPTP

- It does not always deliver a decisive victory for one party or create a strong and stable government. The Conservatives failed to gain an overall majority in both the 2010 and the 2017 general elections.
- It can lead to a situation where the winning MP in a constituency has received less than 30% of the vote. In 2017 the SNP's Stephen Gethins won North East Fife by just two votes over the Liberal Democrats after three recounts.
- The number of seats in the House of Commons does not accurately reflect the percentages of votes for each of the parties. In 2015, UKIP gained 12.6% of the vote but only 1 seat.

Hints & tips

In order to try and remember the arguments for and against FPTP you could try to make up a mnemonic to aid your learning. For example, ***B.E.E.S.***

✓ *By-elections – FPTP allows by-elections*
✓ *Extremist – the system prevents extremist parties*
✓ *Easy – FPTP is easy to understand and simple*
✓ *Strong – the system provides strong government*

Questions and model answers

Describe question

Political parties campaign to get their candidates elected as MPs in a number of ways.

Describe, **in detail**, **two** ways in which political parties campaign to get their candidates elected as MPs. **6 marks**

Hints & tips

✓ *For 6 marks, you must describe* ***two*** *ways in which political parties campaign.*
✓ *Include examples when you can and make sure you fully explain your points.*
✓ *Try to write as much detail as you can in the time given; there are no prizes for finishing first!*

Remember

Knowledge and understanding questions will have 4, 6 or 8 marks allocated and you will need to answer three questions 'describing' or 'explaining'.

Hints & tips

Make sure you take account of how many marks a question is worth. You should base the length of your answers on the time you should allocate to 4-mark, 6-mark and 8-mark questions.

Model answer

Political parties campaign to get their candidates elected in a number of different ways. One way is to canvass voters. Parties will employ a number of volunteers who will work alongside the candidates as they go door-to-door or even telephone households. They canvass voters by discussing the election with them in person and in doing so try to gain their vote.

Another way political parties help in election campaigns is by producing a large variety of promotional materials. This may take the form of leaflets that are delivered through the doors of voters and even huge billboard posters in town centres to promote their candidate. For example, in many constituencies during elections, lamp posts are usually covered in placards with the candidate's name on them, and quite often cars drive around the streets with loudspeakers through which a message is played to support a campaign.

Marker's comment

This is a very good answer because it is relevant and detailed. Each point is fully explained with examples where possible. Each paragraph clearly includes at least one point that addresses the question and the candidate is showing clearly that they understand the question completely. This answer would gain full marks. **6 marks**

Explain question

Many people wish to reform the House of Lords.

Explain, **in detail**, two ways in which people wish to reform the House of Lords. **6 marks**

Model answer

The House of Lords forms part of the UK Parliament, alongside the House of Commons. However, many people believe it to be undemocratic. This is because the House of Lords has power, such as to delay government Bills, but cannot be held responsible by voters because their appointments are for life and they are not elected.

In addition, many people, including the Liberal Democrats, believe that the UK should have an elected second chamber as, for example, in the USA, which has both the Senate and the House of Representatives. Some people believe the House of Lords is outdated and too traditional and does not reflect modern society.

Marker's comments

This answer is very good as it addresses the question directly. It clearly describes ways that the Lords should be reformed. The detail in the answer shows the candidate's knowledge of the main issues with regards to the House of Lords. Added to this, the candidate is able to give two clear examples to back up their points.

This answer would gain full marks. **6 marks**

Hints & tips

- ✓ *For 6 marks, you must come up with two detailed explanations.*
- ✓ *You can gain a maximum of 4 marks for a well developed point, but for the best chance of high marks you should be looking to write three well explained and exemplified points for 6 marks.*
- ✓ *For each point, ensure you use exemplification to enhance your answer.*
- ✓ *Try to write as much detail as you can in the time given; there are no prizes for finishing first!*

Chapter 5
Influence

What you should know 

In class you will have studied either trade unions **OR** pressure groups **AND** the media in either a UK or Scottish context.

To be successful in this section, you should be able to:

★ for **trade unions,** describe and explain the purpose, aims and methods of trade unions

★ for **pressure groups,** describe and explain the purpose, aims and methods of pressure groups

★ for **the media,** describe and explain the ownership and control of media, and the impact of newspapers, television and 'new media'.

Trade unions

Trade unions (TUs) are organisations that represent workers in their place of employment. Trade unions follow the principle of collective bargaining – where a group is more powerful than an individual. An employer is more likely to listen when a group of employees raises an issue than when a single employee does so.

The aims of trade unions

Almost one worker in every five in the UK is a TU member. This equates to around 7 million workers.

Trade unions have the following key aims:

Figure 5.1 The key aims of trade unions

Shop stewards

Shop stewards (also called union representatives) are elected by the union members in a workplace. In the same way that an MP represents the people in a constituency, a union shop steward represents the members of the union and will listen to their concerns and work with the employer to try to resolve them. The shop steward will represent their union members at regional and national meetings of the trade union.

The methods used by trade unions

Trade unions use negotiation to try to change working practices for their members, such as securing better pay deals or improving the working environment. If negotiation fails, they can use a number of forms of industrial action to try to put pressure on an employer to meet their demands. Union members must be balloted before any industrial action can take place, and action can only take place if a majority of those who vote are in favour of it.

Industrial action	What it means
Overtime ban	Members will only work their contracted number of hours.
Go slow	Members will deliberately take more time to do their job and will not attempt to be overly productive.
Work-to-rule	Members will not perform any duties over and above those stated in their contract of employment.
Strike	Members refuse to work in order to put pressure on their employer. This is the most serious action that union members can take. Members will not be paid by the employer during the period of the strike. The threat of a strike can sometimes be enough to gain concessions from an employer.

Table 5.1 Forms of industrial action

Rights and responsibilities of trade unions

Rights

- To take industrial action.
- To recruit new members.
- To be consulted about changes to working conditions by employers.
- To ask about changes to pay and working conditions.

Responsibilities

- To follow the legal procedures and to ensure protests are peaceful.
- Not to force or bully people into joining.
- To ensure they act with their members' consent and do not act in their own interests.
- Not to make unreasonable demands or threaten employers.

Example 1: UK

NHS junior doctor strikes

Throughout 2016, the British Medical Association backed over 20,000 junior doctors in strike action over proposed changes to their contracts in England by the UK Government.

Example 2: Scotland

College lecturers go on a one-day strike

On 27 April 2017, Scottish college lecturers who are members of the EIS (Educational Institute of Scotland) union went on a one-day strike over differences in pay between colleges. They claimed that the colleges had not honoured a deal that was agreed to equalise pay.

Pressure groups

A pressure group is a group of people who work together to try to influence public opinion and government policy on a particular issue. There are thousands of pressure groups in the UK working on a range of causes, including human rights, food, animal welfare and the environment. Some pressure groups are large international organisations; others are small, local campaigns, such as a protest over plans to close a school.

The aims of pressure groups

Some pressure groups will have a single aim; others will have several aims, but they are always directly related to the issue involved. The North Kelvin Meadow Campaign is a community group in the West End of Glasgow that campaigns for an area of green space near Maryhill to be retained as a multi-use community area. In contrast, the Countryside Alliance works on a range of issues, including the promotion of hunting, shooting and rural life.

There are two types of pressure group: cause groups and sectional groups. Cause (or promotional) pressure groups promote a particular cause, while sectional pressure groups represent the interests of a group or section of society.

Cause groups	Sectional groups
Membership is open to anyone who supports the cause.	Membership is restricted to the people whose interests the group represents, such as teachers or nurses.
Groups may be small and may be temporary – they may only exist for as long as the cause exists. Others may have been established for a long time and may have a huge membership. Some of these groups are registered charities.	Groups are well organised and campaign on the issues that affect their members. They can threaten industrial action in order to achieve their aims.
Examples: **Greenpeace** – campaigns on a global scale on environmental issues. **Amnesty International** – a multi-national group that campaigns for human rights.	Examples: **BMA (British Medical Association)** – represents the interests of doctors. **Unison** – the UK's largest public sector worker trade union, which represents NHS staff and civil servants.

Table 5.2 Cause and sectional pressure groups

The methods used by pressure groups

Contact representatives	Pressure groups: • contact their representatives, for example MPs, MSPs or councillors, to draw attention to the subject • ask for support and public acknowledgement of support by backing a campaign • try to persuade the representative to vote the preferred way in Parliament over the subject.
Draw up petitions	Pressure groups often draw up petitions to gain public support in order to show that members of the public have strong feelings about the issue. Petitions are often signed in public areas, such as town centres, or can be supported through online petitions or social media such as Facebook and Twitter.
Organise public protests	Pressure groups often organise public protests to support their causes and these can be marches, demonstrations or rallies. Public protests generally make the local or national news and are a good way of getting attention for the issue.
Create campaigns to suit the issue	Pressure groups use different styles of campaign to gain support, depending on the type of issue: • leaflets can be posted through letter boxes in residential areas or handed out in public areas • posters can be displayed in appropriate areas • the internet, and social media such as Facebook and Twitter, are used by pressure groups such as Amnesty International.
Mass media	Pressure groups use mass media, such as newspapers, television and radio, to promote their causes. • News items or advertisements can be placed in newspapers or magazines to promote the issue and gain support. • Guests could appear on television or radio programmes, or as panellists on current events or news programmes.

Table 5.3 Methods used by pressure groups

Rights and responsibilities of pressure groups

Rights

- To protest, through marches, demonstrations and industrial action.
- To promote their cause using mass media and new media.
- To actively try to recruit new members.
- To contact representatives to try to gain their support.
- To organise petitions to show public support.

Responsibilities

- To protest legally and peacefully.
- Not to slander individuals or tell lies in order to try to persuade people to support the cause.
- Not to force people to join the group, or bully or intimidate people who oppose their aims.
- Not to intimidate politicians, or threaten blackmail to further their cause.
- Not to falsify signatures. Support for the cause must be genuine.

Example 1: UK

Jamie Oliver's Food Revolution

Following Jamie Oliver's successful Feed Me Better campaign in 2005 which forced wholesale change to school meals across England, he founded the Food Revolution campaign which aims to put pressure on the Government and businesses over the growing issue of childhood obesity. One victory has been the promise to introduce a tax on sugary drinks.

Example 2: Scotland

Faslane peace camp

For 30 years there has been an anti-nuclear protest camp outside the gates of Faslane Naval Base, which is situated on the Gare Loch to the north of the River Clyde. The base contains the UK's nuclear Trident submarines.

The media

Media is the different ways that information is communicated to the public and includes newspapers (print media), radio and television (broadcast media) and the internet (new media). Today, social media is another important means of communication of news and information.

The media has three roles in society:

- to entertain
- to educate
- to inform.

By controlling the information that is communicated, the media can shape our attitudes and opinions. The UK has a **free press**, which means that the media can criticise the Government and political parties, and politicians will aim to keep the media 'on their side' so that they do not receive negative press coverage.

Key words

Free press: Media that is not restricted or censored by the government.

Newspapers

Newspapers are classified as 'tabloids' (such as the *Daily Mail* and the *Daily Record*) or 'broadsheets' (such as *The Telegraph* and *The Herald*).

Most newspapers favour a particular political party and the stories that they print will tend to reflect favourably on that party. For example, the *Daily Mail* is known to support the Conservative Party and will print stories that show Theresa May in a positive light. At the same time, they will print stories that show the other political parties in a bad light. In this way newspapers can shape our attitudes and opinions about political parties and can encourage us to vote for a particular party in an election.

Newspapers and elections

Politicians understand the importance of having the support of the media. Over 12 million people buy a newspaper every day in the UK – that is a lot of potential voters that a newspaper can influence.

In 1992, *The Sun*, Britain's biggest selling daily newspaper, gave its support to the Conservative Party and when the Conservatives won the general election the newspaper declared 'It's the Sun wot won it'. The newspaper switched to support the Labour Party in the 1997 election and declared 'The Sun backs Blair', but in the run up to the 2010 election it returned to support the Conservatives, announcing 'Labour's lost it.' Other national newspapers also moved their support from the Labour Party, who went on to lose power to the Conservatives. *The Sun* continued to support the Conservatives during the 2017 general election.

In Scotland, the SNP did not have the full support of any national newspaper before the 2007 Scottish Parliament elections. The Party won the election but only won enough votes to form a minority government. In the run up to the 2011 election the party gained the backing of the *Scottish Sun* newspaper and this time won enough votes in the election to form a majority government. It retained the newspaper's support in the 2016 Scottish Parliament elections.

The overall influence of newspapers should not be exaggerated, but the evidence shows that having the support of a major national newspaper does not harm a party at election time.

Television

While newspapers can support a political party, broadcast media – television and radio – must follow strict broadcasting guidelines and remain **politically impartial**. There is an independent body, called Ofcom, responsible for making sure that television channels are not biased towards any political party or agenda and that their reporting is neutral.

Key words

Politically impartial: Does not favour any one political party and provides a balanced opinion.

Television and elections

The run up to the 2010 general election was the first time that televised leaders' debates had taken place in the UK. (This is a common occurrence during election campaigns in the USA.) The leaders of the three main parties – Nick Clegg (Liberal Democrats), David Cameron (Conservatives) and Gordon Brown (Labour) – took part in three debates broadcast, in turn, by ITV, BSkyB and the BBC.

Figure 5.2 The 2010 televised leaders' debates

In the 2017 general election Theresa May bucked the trend and refused to appear on TV debates. Many commentators claim that this directly impacted the result: the Conservatives lost their majority and there was a hung parliament.

Televised debates were also held in Scotland for the first time in the run up to the 2011 Scottish Parliament elections. The leaders of the four main parties took part in the debates – Alex Salmond (SNP), Iain Gray (Labour), Annabel Goldie (Conservatives) and Tavish Scott (Liberal Democrats).

These TV debates have continued up to the most recent election, during which Nicola Sturgeon was praised for her performance and was even named Politician of the Year by *The Herald* newspaper in 2015.

New media and the internet

The internet and social media now play a major role in the communication of information. Like newspapers, websites are not required to be politically impartial and they can show support for a particular party. Political parties use their websites and social media pages to engage voters (particularly younger voters) and generate support.

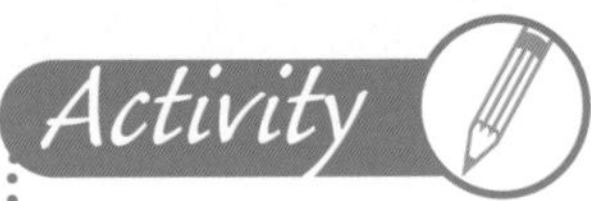

Research how a political party might use social media during an election campaign.

Control of the media

The Press Complaints Commission (PCC) is an independent body that deals with complaints about things written in newspapers and magazines. Journalists and newspapers must follow its **code of practice** and not publish incorrect or misleading information about people, companies, groups or political parties.

Key words

Code of practice: A set of guidelines that must be followed, e.g. for newspapers on acceptable reporting.

Leveson Inquiry

In 2012, an independent inquiry (called the Leveson Inquiry) was held into the freedom of the press. The inquiry was the result of allegations of phone hacking of celebrities and members of the public by the (now defunct) *News of the World* newspaper. Following the inquiry, a cross-party agreement for a Royal Charter was announced in early 2013. The charter will protect the freedom of the press and at the same time protect the public from the kinds of abuses that made the Leveson Inquiry necessary. There will be a new independent self-regulatory body that will deal fairly with complaints and ensure that newspapers print apologies on their front page if they publish statements that are proven to be inaccurate. The body will be able to mount investigations and, where appropriate, impose meaningful sanctions on inaccurate reporting.

Who owns the media?

The BBC is paid for by a licence fee that everyone in the UK must pay if they own a television. BSkyB is owned by several shareholders, including Rupert Murdoch (39%). In 2017 the regulator approved the takeover of BSkyB by Fox News, a News Corporation company. Rupert Murdoch's News Corporation company also owns *The Sun* and *The Times* newspapers, which means he has a lot of influence over the media in the UK.

Part Three: Social Issues in the UK

This section of the book provides summary course notes for the Social Issues in the UK Section of the course.

You will have studied one of the following topics as part of your National 5 Social Issues Section:

- Social Inequality, or
- Crime and the Law.

In the knowledge section of the exam you will answer **three questions** on this Section and these questions will be allocated 4, 6 or 8 marks each.

Chapter 6

Social Inequality

What you should know

To be successful in this section, you should **know** and **understand**:

- ★ the nature of social inequality:
  - the extent of social inequality in Scotland and/or the UK
  - the evidence (official reports/academic research) of social inequality in Scotland and/or the UK
- ★ the causes of social and economic inequality:
  - employment/unemployment
  - income
  - educational attainment
  - discrimination
- ★ the consequences of social and economic inequality for:
  - individuals
  - families
  - communities
  - wider society
- ★ the responses to social inequality and the effectiveness of the:
  - government response
  - private sector response
  - voluntary sector response
- ★ the impact of social and economic inequalities on at least **two** of the following groups:
  - social class
  - age
  - gender
  - minority groups.

Evidence of social and economic inequality

Income and poverty

Table 6.1 shows the percentages and numbers of individuals, children, working-age adults and pensioners living in **relative** and **absolute poverty** in Scotland in 2014 and 2016. There are no considerable changes between the two dates.

Key words

Relative poverty is if you live in a household with an income 60% below the median income. A couple with two children are living in poverty if they are living on less than £355 a week.

Absolute poverty is a measure of whether the income of the poorest households are keeping pace with inflation.

	Relative poverty		Absolute poverty	
	2016	2014	2016	2014
All individuals	20% (1.05 million)	18%	18% (960,000)	17%
Children	26% (260,000)	22%	24% (230,000)	24%
Working-age adults	20% (650,000)	19%	19% (610,000)	19%

Table 6.1 Relative and absolute poverty after housing costs (Scotland, 2016 and 2014)

- **In-work poverty**
  - 66% of children who experience relative poverty live in in-work families (significant change – it was 45% in 2000)
- **Pensioner poverty**
  - 13% of pensioners – 140,000 people are in relative poverty – no change from 2000
  - 12% of pensioners – 120,000 people are in absolute poverty – no change from 2000

Income inequality

- The top 10% of the Scottish population had 38% more income than the bottom 40% combined. (An income of £47,500 would be in the top 10%.)
- Lone parents' income has fallen and as such relative poverty has increased in recent years from 24% to 31%.

The Gini coefficient measures the degree of inequality in household income. In 2016 the UK figure stood at 34, an increase from 31 in 2014.

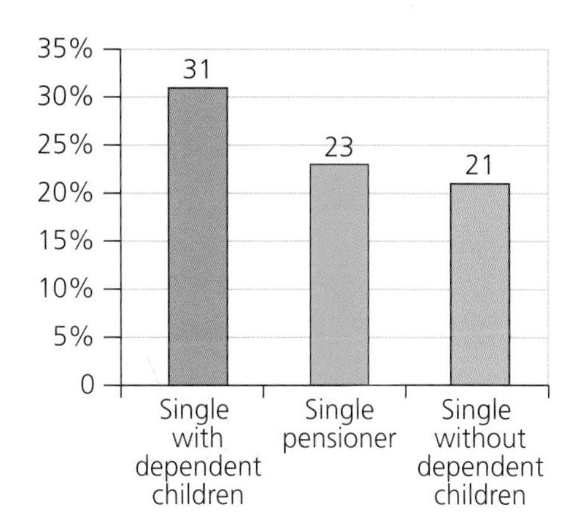

Figure 6.1 The three top households experiencing poverty (%), 2017

Causes of social and economic inequality

Social exclusion

Being poor impacts on individuals' and families' involvement in their community. Their children may not be able to participate in many activities such as school trips. This can affect their self-esteem and contribute towards a cycle of poverty. Individuals and families may experience a feeling of hopelessness and have low expectations of living a meaningful life. Ethnic minorities also experience **social exclusion** due to discrimination, racism and poor housing.

Key words

Social exclusion is the impact of poverty on individuals and groups and the extent to which they are unable to participate in aspects of society such as education, health and housing due to being in poverty.

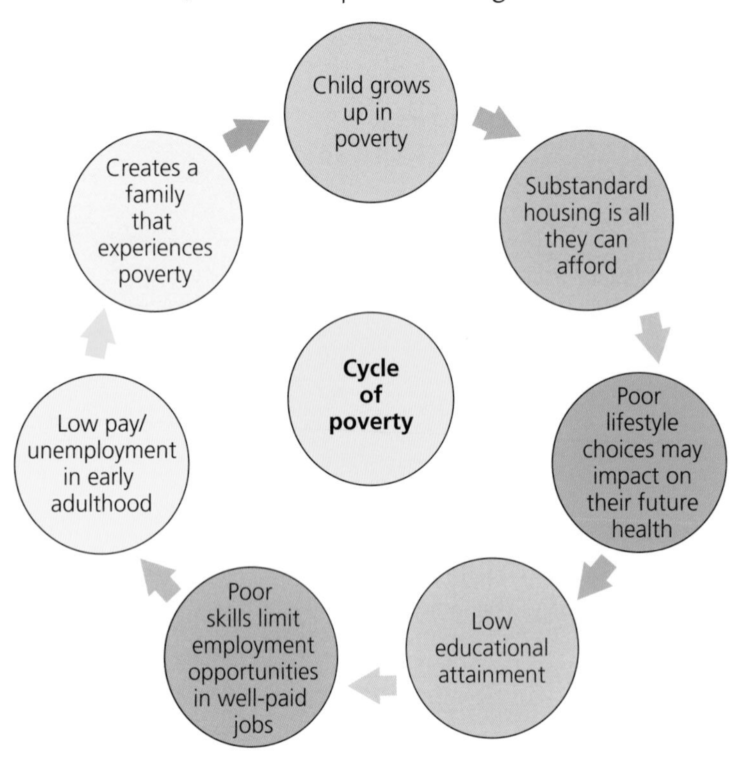

Fig 6.2 The cycle of poverty

Unemployment, low pay and the benefits system

The Government believes that work is the best way out of poverty as it can end the generational cycle of unemployment. The Conservative reforms to the benefits system (see page 45) are based on providing 'incentives' to unemployed individuals to move from welfare to work. The unemployment rate in the UK has fallen from 8.2% in 2012 to 4.6% in 2017, but poverty has not declined.

Key words

A **zero-hour contract** is a form of employment contract under which an employer does not have to state how many hours the employee will work per week. Employers do not need to pay pension contributions or redundancy pay.

Why has poverty not decreased?

- Most of the new jobs are low paid, especially with the massive increase in employers using **zero-hour contracts**. Since the Conservatives came to power in 2010, the number of workers on these contracts has increased from 168,000 to over 900,000 by the end of 2016. If you are unemployed and refuse to accept a zero-hour contract, your benefit payments will be stopped. These contracts provide flexibility to students and retired workers but create job insecurity and very low salaries for workers looking for a permanent protected work contract.

- This has led to a significant increase in the number of working poor, especially those with families.
- The banking and economic crisis has led to a significant decrease in government spending on welfare, as outlined below.
- Many benefits have been frozen or increased below the rate of inflation.
- In 2013 the Government limited the amount a family could receive on welfare benefit. This is called the benefit cap. In 2016 this figure was further lowered to £20,000 (£23,000 in London). This will reduce about 10,000 Scottish household incomes by an average of £57 per week; 80% of the households hit by these cuts are lone-parent families.
- UK housing benefit has been reduced if your house is under-occupied. This has been called the bedroom tax.
- Harsh sanctions have been introduced for those who break Jobcentre guidelines.

Consequences of social and economic inequality

Health inequalities

- Men born in Scotland's most affluent areas live over twelve years longer than those in the poorest areas – 82.4 years life expectancy compared to 69.9 years.
- British Heart Foundation statistics confirm that people in Glasgow have the highest rate of deaths from heart disease in the UK. In Glasgow 144 people out of every 100,000 die from heart disease compared to only 40 per 100,000 in wealthy parts of the south of England.
- Office for National Statistics (ONS) figures show that Scotland has the highest male rate of alcohol-rated deaths in the UK: 29.1 per 100,000 compared to 17.8 per 100,000 in England.
- Scotland's drug problem is reflected by the scandal of 700 babies born addicted to hard drugs between 2012 and 2016.
- People in the most deprived communities are more likely to smoke, drink and suffer from obesity than those in less deprived areas; for example, a Scottish government smoking survey discovered that 34% of people in the most deprived areas smoked compared to just 9% of those in the least deprived areas.
- Children and adults from low-income families are nearly three times more likely to suffer mental health problems than those from more affluent households.

Poverty or lifestyle choices

One view is that lifestyle choices, rather than poverty, create poor health. The individual chooses to smoke, drink too much and have an unhealthy diet. This is too simplistic, however, as evidence shows a clear link between poverty and poor lifestyle choices. Poor housing and low income reduces the opportunities that many of us take for granted and can lead to depression.

Educational inequalities

- A Primary 1 pupil from the poorest communities in Scotland is more than a year behind better-off pupils.
- More than half of the bottom 20% of Primary 4 pupils come from the three most deprived local authorities.
- In 2014, 1335 school-leavers from the poorest 20% of households went to university in Scotland compared to 5520 from the richest 20% of communities.

Fuel poverty and poor housing

Many poor people suffer from poorly insulated homes and find it difficult to heat their homes in winter time. This can have a serious impact on health, especially for children and the elderly.

Elderly inequalities

- Many pensioners, especially women, do not have a private pension as they may have worked in low-paid or part-time employment.
- Those who were unemployed during much of their working lives will not have a private pension.
- There are significant income and quality-of-life inequalities between those who depend solely on a state pension and those with a private pension.
- 1 million out of 4 million single pensioners are entirely dependent on the state pension and, as such, live in poverty.

Social inequality: gender and ethnicity

- Both women and people from ethnic minorities have made progress towards greater equality in the workplace through legislation and changing attitudes, but much has still to be done.
- Men are twice as likely as women to be employed in a top job and, on average, men earn 9% more than women.
- It is estimated that about 40% of the black and minority ethnic (BME) population live on a low income – twice the rate of white British people.
- The youth unemployment rate for non-Asian BMEs is almost twice the rate for white 16–24 year olds.

Barrier	Explanation
Glass ceiling	A term to describe the invisible barrier that stops women and other disadvantaged groups from being promoted to senior management posts, despite their qualifications and/or achievements.
Low-paid sector of the economy	Women tend to be concentrated in the low-paid 'four Cs': catering, cleaning, caring and cashier work.
Child care and part-time work	Women with young children may find it more convenient to work part-time and are far more likely than men to take career breaks.
Discrimination and stereotyping	Some employers may prefer to employ men for certain jobs and ethnic minorities feel they are discriminated against when they apply for employment.

Table 6.2 Barriers to achieving equality

Responses to social and economic inequality

The Welfare State

Both the UK and Scottish Governments have the responsibility of protecting the health and wellbeing of its citizens, especially those who are ill, on a low income or part of a vulnerable group. The generous use of tax credits in the UK has helped to reduce the number of families living below the poverty line from 35% in 1999 to 19% by 2012.

In Scotland the threshold for paying the 40p rate of income tax is frozen at £43,000; this is in contrast to the rest of the UK, where it is at £45,000. This means that some Scottish taxpayers pay £400 more tax than those outside Scotland and this extra income can help to tackle inequalities.

Benefit/policy	Impact
National Living Wage	Introduced in April 2016 by the Conservative Government, this replaces the National Minimum Wage for all workers aged 25 or over. The wage will begin at £7.20 an hour and benefits around 2.7 million workers. This is, however, lower than the Living Wage.
Child Benefit	This is paid to those who have a child or children under the age of sixteen or under the age of twenty in education. Families with one individual earning £60,000 are not entitled to this benefit. However, this benefit has been frozen and is declining in real terms.
Universal Credit	This combines six benefits into one payment and encourages individuals to take greater responsibility for managing their budgets. It is easier to understand and cheaper to administer than the individual benefits. It is being phased in across the UK. However, payments are made monthly and many unemployed people are falling into debt. In areas that have implemented Universal Credit, rent arrears have significantly increased.
Tax credits	Working Tax Credit and Child Tax Credit have helped to improve the living standards of individuals and families. They have especially helped one-parent families – 194,000 working families receive tax credits, and more than half of these are lone parents. From 2017 Child Tax Credit will only be available for the first two children, which will affect up to 800,000 families. Families with three children, who are receiving the Child Tax Credit, could lose about £2,870 a year.
Other family benefits	These include maternity grants and free school meals.
Job Seeker's Allowance and Jobcentre Plus	Jobcentre Plus aims to find people work by giving advice about job application and interviews. However, if an unemployed person breaks the rules they will be sanctioned and will not receive welfare benefits for a set period. This can create fuel and food poverty.
Support for pensioners	The state pension is paid to those who have reached retirement age. The Winter Fuel Payment is also available to all pensioners. The means-tested benefits of Pension Credit and Cold Weather Payments are also available to some. Since 2010 the state pension has been protected to ensure that it rises in line with prices, earnings or 2.5%, whichever is the greater. (This is called triple lock protection.)

Table 6.3 Some of the main benefits and policies

The Scottish dimension

- The Scottish Government now has responsibility for some welfare payments and can take some action to protect vulnerable people.
- The 2016 Scottish Social Security Bill abolished the bedroom tax and increased the Carer's Allowance. This helps to alleviate poverty for the disabled in particular.

MS Society says many sufferers lost benefits in payment switch

Thousands of people disabled by multiple sclerosis have seen their benefits cut since the Disability Living Allowance (DLA) began to be replaced by the Personal Independence Payment (PIP) in 2013.

The MS Society revealed that one in three people who had previously received the highest rate mobility component of DLA – around 2600 people across the UK – had their payment downgraded or denied after being reassessed for PIP between October 2013 and October 2016.

Scotland has been the worst hit as the prevalence of MS is much higher there than in other parts of the UK.

Scottish Government response to educational inequalities

- **Educational Maintenance Allowance (EMA)** If you are between sixteen and nineteen years old in a school or college and come from a low-income family you will receive a grant. (The EMA has been scrapped in England.)
- **Scottish Pupil Equity Fund** In 2017 the Scottish Government allocated £120 million to 2300 schools as part of the Scottish Pupil Equity Fund. The aim of the fund is to close the poverty-related attainment gap. The amount a school receives depends on levels of deprivation, calculated on free school meal entitlement. St Andrew's Secondary in Glasgow received the largest individual award of £354,000.
- Scottish students do not pay tuition fees; in England universities can charge fees of up to £9000 per year.
- The Scottish Government target is for 20% of all those starting university in 2030 to be from the poorest 20% of the community. The interim target is 10% by 2021.
- Young people from deprived backgrounds who receive the minimum grades required are given entry to university courses. Some argue this discriminates against middle-class students.
- The proportion of applicants to university from the 40% most deprived backgrounds has risen from 28% to 39%.
- Some universities offer scholarships worth up to £2000 a year to students from poor households and offer outreach projects to encourage those from poor backgrounds to consider university.

Government responses to health inequalities

- The ban on smoking in public places was introduced in 2006, and in 2017 it became illegal to smoke in a car with someone under the age of eighteen present.
- Prescriptions and eye tests are free in Scotland.
- In 2016 the Scottish Government set up Food Standards Scotland (FSS) to work with health experts to prepare a levy on sugar products. Any such tax would need the approval of Westminster.
- NHS Scotland claims that UK welfare cuts are undermining efforts to improve the nation's health. They argue that there is a link between the rise in mental health problems and the introduction of tougher sanctions for those deemed to have broken job-seeking rules.
- **Free vitamins** In March 2017 the expansion of the UK-wide Health Start voucher scheme changed in Scotland from a means-tested benefit to a universal benefit for all pregnant women. They will all receive the recommended dosages of vitamins C, D and folic acid at an estimated cost of £300,000 per year.
- **Baby Box** From August 2017 all parents of new babies will be offered a free baby box, worth £160, based on a Finnish initiative. It will contain items such as clothes, blankets and toys, and the box can be used as a baby's crib. It is hoped that this initiative will reduce infant mortality.
- The Scottish death rate for heart disease has fallen by 43% in the past decade in both affluent and poor areas.
- Scottish deaths caused by alcohol have fallen for women from 17.3 per 100,000 in 2004 to 13 per 100,000 in 2015.
- There has been a significant drop in the number of adults smoking in Scotland. In a 2016 government survey only 20% of adults said they smoked compared to 23% in 2013.

Government responses to gender and ethnicity inequality

- The UK Equality Act 2010 brought together the previous nine pieces of equality legislation covering gender, race and disability. Equal pay for equal work, even if different roles are being carried out, must be adhered to.
- The Equality and Human Rights Commission monitors and reports on pay division between races and gender in unrepresentative public bodies.
- A UK cabinet minister has responsibility for gender and minorities and this places equality issues at the heart of the Government.
- The Scottish Government has set a target of a 50:50 gender balance on public sector boards by 2020. The Scottish cabinet has a gender balance and until August 2017 all the leaders of the Scottish three main political parties were women.
- Large companies are encouraged to publish data on gender wage differences. In July 2017 the BBC was forced to publish their high-earning employees' salaries which highlighted a significant gender pay gap.

- The introduction of the Minimum Wage (now replaced by the Living Wage), Working Tax Credits and Child Tax Credits have increased the income of the lowest wage earners in society. As many female and ethnic minority workers suffer from low-income employment, these policies have been of great benefit to these two groups.

Effectiveness of private sector response

Over recent years controversial contracts have been given to private firms to administer government reforms of welfare payments to the disabled. All recipients of the Disability Living Allowance are having their health disabilities reassessed before moving on to the new benefit of the Personal Independence Payment (PIP). Many ill people have suffered distress and financial hardship as the private firm has decided that they are fit for work and, as a result, they have had their benefits reduced.

Private health firms

- Help to reduce waiting lists by carrying out operations on behalf of the NHS. In 2016 Scottish health boards paid private firms a record £82.5 million. (The figure has doubled since 2000.) Critics argue that this is wasteful as costs are higher in the private sector.
- PFI (Private Finance Initiative) has enabled some health boards to build state-of-the-art hospitals such as the Edinburgh Royal Infirmary (ERI). However, these contracts are now costing Health Boards £260 million a year. The ERI cost the private sector £184 million to build but the overall cost to NHS Lothian will be a staggering £1.6 billion.

Voluntary organisations

Many voluntary and private groups work in partnership with local and central government to provide help to those in need. Organisations such as Oxfam and the Joseph Rowntree Foundation raise money for projects to help people in poverty. Food companies also provide surplus food to food banks around Britain. Below are some of the actions taken by voluntary groups:

- The Scottish Council for Voluntary Organisations (SCVO) acts as a pressure group to highlight the impact of welfare reforms and to provide support to those in need.
- Citizens Advice Scotland (CAS) has called for a review of cash penalties being imposed on the unemployed – a deprived area of Glasgow has seen a 400% rise in sanctions. It is estimated that 73% of referrals to food banks are for people or families affected by benefit delays and sanctions.
- Child Poverty Action Group (CPAG) highlights the impact of welfare reforms on the plight of the poor and families. In autumn 2017, CPAG, supported by charities and churches, launched its campaign for an additional £5 per child per week to be given to families that receive Child Benefit. The campaign entitled 'Give Me Five' is in response to the Government's decision to freeze Child Benefit. CPAG argues that child poverty is increasing.

Questions and model answers

Remember

Knowledge and understanding questions will have 4, 6 or 8 marks allocated and you will need to answer three questions.

Remember

In a describe question, up to 3 marks can be awarded for each description you make, depending on its quality, level of detail, relevance, accuracy and exemplification.

Describe question

Living in poverty can have a severe impact on families.

Describe, **in detail**, **two** ways in which poverty can have a severe impact on families. **4 marks**

Model answer

One impact of poverty is that families may live in a sub-standard house and in a challenging area. They might experience fuel poverty and find it difficult to heat their homes properly which can lead to dampness.

Families living in poverty may have a poor diet of cheap foods such as tinned or ready meals. They might not get a balanced diet as fruit and vegetables are expensive to buy. This can lead to problems of obesity, especially for children.

Marker's comment

In this answer, two factors are described. The first paragraph would receive 2 marks because it accurately identifies the link between poverty and inadequate housing and the inability to heat their home.

The second paragraph would easily get 2 marks because it accurately identifies the link between poverty and poor diet which can lead to obesity.

Overall a high-quality answer deserving of full marks. **4 marks**

Explain question

Health inequalities exist in the UK.

Explain, **in detail**, **two** reasons why health inequalities still exist in the UK. **6 marks**

Model answer

There is a clear link between living in a poor area and having poorer health than someone who lives in a more affluent area. Living in poor housing with possible dampness, and lacking money to afford a balanced diet can damage one's health. Being unemployed can lead to depression and impact on health. In contrast, someone living in an affluent area is more likely to live in a warm house, eat a balance diet and exercise.

Health inequalities also exist because many people make poor lifestyle choices. Choosing to smoke, excessively drinking alcohol and eating a poor diet can lead to serious health problems such as diabetes.

Marker's comment

In this answer the first paragraph would receive 4 marks because in the first sentence it accurately links living in a poor area to social and economic inequalities. This is developed in detail with reference to dampness, unemployment and depression, and a contrast is provided with those living in an affluent area.

The second paragraph would easily get 2 marks (maximum number of marks available) because it accurately identifies lifestyle choices as a key factor. This is developed with reference to smoking, alcohol and poor diet.

Overall, a very good and high-quality answer deserving of full marks. **6 marks**

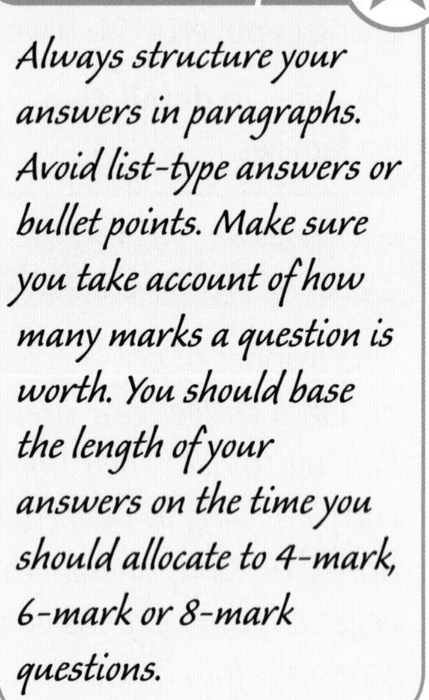

Remember

For a 6-mark answer you must cover at least two factors in depth. In an explain question, a maximum of 4 marks can be given for each detailed point you give, depending on their quality, level of detail, relevance, accuracy and exemplification. In your answer, it is also good to show the interaction of various factors.

Chapter 7
Crime and the Law

What you should know

To be successful in this section, you should be able to:

- ★ **describe** and **explain** the:
  - nature and extent of crime in Scotland and/or the UK
  - evidence of crime in Scotland and/or the UK, such as official reports and academic research
- ★ **know** and **understand** the causes of and explanations for crime:
  - social
  - economic
  - biological
- ★ **know** and **understand** the consequences of crime for:
  - perpetrators
  - victims
  - families
  - communities
  - wider society
- ★ **describe** and **explain** the criminal justice system, including the:
  - role and structure of the criminal courts (including the Children's Hearings System)
  - powers of the criminal court (including the Children's Hearings System)
  - effectiveness of criminal courts in tackling crime
- ★ **describe** and **explain** the responses to crime, including:
  - government responses and their effectiveness
  - the role, structure and powers of the police in Scotland and their effectiveness in tackling crime
  - the purpose and effectiveness of prison and alternatives to prison
- ★ **know** and **understand** the impact of crime and law on at least **two** of the following groups:
  - social class
  - age
  - gender
  - minority groups.

The nature of crime

Crime takes place when the laws of a country are broken. New laws are continually being passed to reflect changing social values and threats to society such as cybercrime. Law and order is the responsibility of the

Scottish Parliament and laws have been introduced in Scotland, such as the recent drink driving laws, which are different from those in England. Crime can vary from the most serious such as murder or rape to lesser crimes such as shoplifting.

Different types of crime

Violent crime

Robbery is different from theft if it involves taking something from a person by force or by the threat of force, and is a form of assault. Rape, knife crime and domestic violence are all examples of violent crime.

White-collar crime

This is described as 'a crime committed by a person of respectability in the course of his/her occupation'. It includes bribery and fraud. These can be hidden crimes as firms often prefer to sack a person to avoid publicity.

Blue-collar crime

This refers to crimes committed by working-class people who perform manual work, such as a lorry driver. Their crimes are more obvious than white-collar crimes and include housebreaking, vandalism and selling stolen goods.

Drug and alcohol crimes

These crimes are often associated with anti-social behaviour as people may only commit the crimes due to the effects of drugs or alcohol. Drug trafficking is a major criminal offence and it is a crime to possess illegal drugs.

Racial crimes

Actions that are racially motivated and which involve abusive and threatening language or acts of violence can carry stiffer sentences than a crime committed with no racial motives.

Evidence of crime

Recorded crime in Scotland is declining, with the figures in 2016 being the lowest since 1974. The official Scottish government statistics (see below) show a total of 246,243 crimes recorded by Police Scotland. There was a worrying increase in sexual crimes, although this included a number of historical cases. The Scottish trends are part of an overall UK drop in crime.

Summary of National Statistics of Crime in Scotland, 2016–17

- Crimes such as vandalism and fire-raising decreased by 3% from the previous year and are at their second lowest level since they peaked in 2006–07.

- A total of 10,822 sexual crimes were recorded – an increase of 5% on the previous year.
- Non-sexual crimes of violence increased by 6% from the previous year to 7164.
- Other crimes fell by 7%.
- Handling offensive weapons increased by 5% from the previous year, but this crime has decreased by 64% over the past ten years.
- Since 2007–08, most types of crime have fallen, for example non-sexual crimes of violence have fallen by 44%, but sexual crime has increased by 65%.

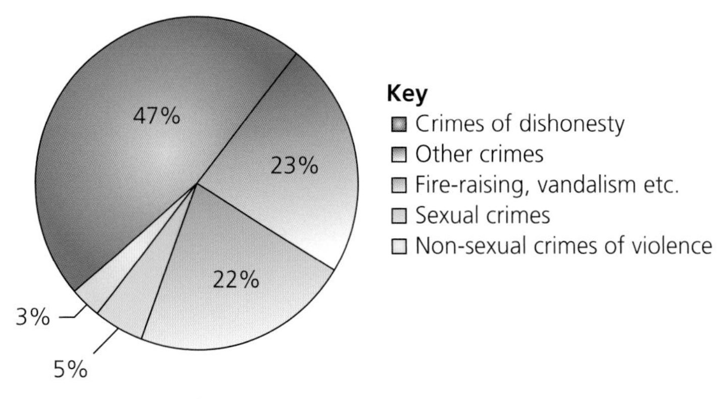

Figure 7.1 Types of recorded crime in Scotland 2016/17

What are the causes of crime?

The causes of crime can be complex, as Figure 7.2 illustrates, and it is therefore useful to use three categories of causes:

- economic
- social
- biological.

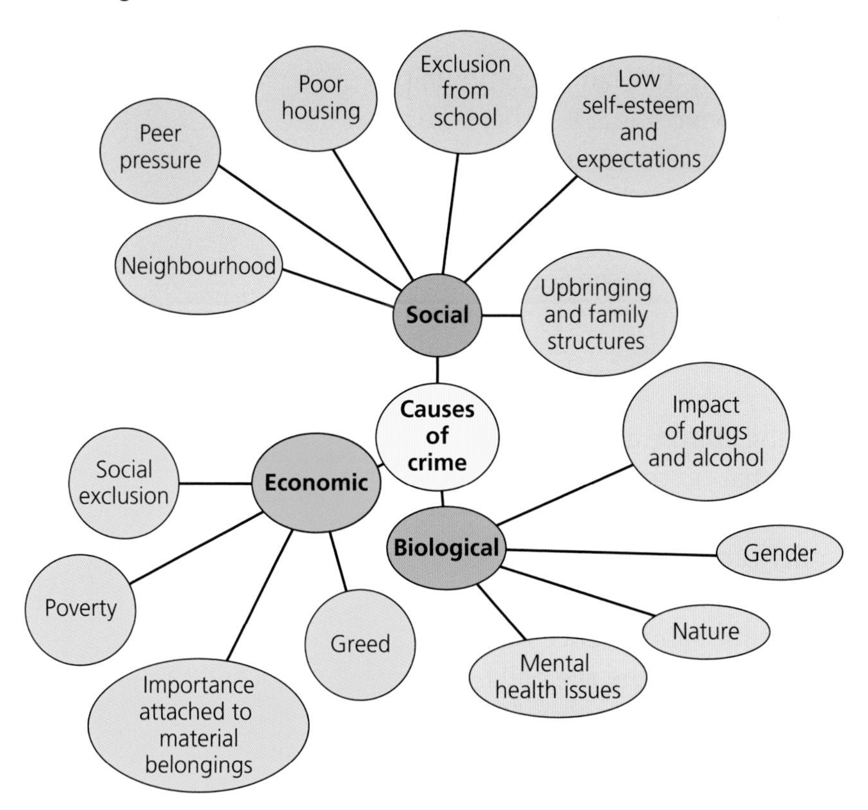

Figure 7.2 Causes of crime

Explanation of economic causes

Poverty

While there is no direct link between poverty and crime, evidence would suggest that those who are poor may be tempted to commit crime. Those who experience social exclusion are more likely to suffer from alcohol/drug addiction, poor mental health and homelessness.

Scotland's most deprived areas have the highest rates of violent crime. Half the prison population comes from home addresses in 155 of the 1222 local government wards in Scotland and these 155 wards are all deprived areas.

However, this does not explain why many relatively well-off individuals commit white-collar crimes. One view is that we live in a materialistic society where one's worth is based on wealth. This fuels greed and envy.

Found guilty of stealing £60,000 from his mother

A retired police officer was found guilty in August 2017 at Stirling Sheriff Court of taking £60,000 from his mother's bank account. She had given him permission to use her card to buy her shopping and to take money out of her account for her personal use. The 86-year-old was shocked when a cheque from her account was rejected by the bank and she contacted the police. Her son and daughter-in-law had used the money to purchase a larger house, luxury cars and to go on an expensive holiday. It was a crime rooted in greed.

Explanation of social causes

Individuals are shaped by their experiences within their family, community and friendship groups and by their socio-economic status. It is therefore a complex combination of factors which lead people to commit crimes. Urban areas with high levels of deprivation often experience a breakdown in the social structure and in institutions such as the family, which can lead to poor attendance at school. This creates an environment ripe for deviant behaviour which leads to hot-spots of crime.

Peer pressure

Young people are also associated with gang culture and the impact of peer pressure. Recent studies have found that up to 3500 young people between the ages of 11 and 23 have joined one of the 170 street gangs within Glasgow's borders. Gangs can offer protection, status, conformity, a sense of community and excitement. According to the Scottish Government, in 2015 42% of all crimes and offences in Scotland were attributable to young people under the age of 21. Young people are responsible for higher proportions of offences such as fire-raising, vandalism, theft of motor vehicles and handling of offensive weapons.

Lack of education

There is a link between poor educational attainment and committing crime. Those who leave school without qualifications find it difficult to find employment. Children who are excluded from school are at risk of drifting into a life of crime.

Explanation of biological causes

Are some individuals born evil or is it the environment they grow up in that makes them carry out violent acts? This is referred to as the nature vs nurture debate. A particularly shocking example of a crime that stimulated this debate was the murder of a toddler, James Bulger, in 1993 in Merseyside. Two ten-year-olds, Robert Thompson and Jon Venables, were charged and found guilty of his murder. The tabloid press labeled them 'sons of Satan', but their family backgrounds displayed classic 'risk factors' – chaotic lifestyle, poverty, alcoholism, marital breakdown, neglect and bullying.

Impact of drugs and alcohol

Alcohol abuse is linked to many crimes, especially violent crimes. Nearly half of all of Scotland's prisoners say that they are under the influence of alcohol at the time of their offence. Drugs also account for 29% of violent crimes. Drug abusers are also more likely to commit crimes such as burglary and muggings in order to fund their habit.

Gender differences

For every 100 crimes committed in Scotland, 88 will be by a man and 12 by a woman. When it comes to violent crime the difference is far higher – only 4 women to 96 men. Women tend to commit low-level, non-violent offences such as shoplifting. This can be explained through biological differences between men and women. As a result of hormonal differences, women tend to be less aggressive as they have lower testosterone levels.

Mental health issues

It is estimated that around 70% of prisoners have mental health issues. Evidence therefore suggests a link between imprisonment and those with conditions such as ADHD (attention deficit hyperactivity disorder) and depression.

Consequences of crime

Impact of crime on offenders and their families

Committing a crime and receiving a prison sentence can have huge personal consequences for offenders and their families. Once released, many convicted criminals find life extremely difficult:

- Offenders often experience unemployment and difficulty in finding work because of their criminal record.

- They may find they are homeless, having lost their homes while in prison.
- They may experience marital difficulties as a result of the stress of their imprisonment and separation from their children.
- Families may experience shame and be rejected by the community in which they live.

Impact of crime on victims and their families

Crime has a huge impact on the individuals involved. Even if victims are not subject to physical harm, the emotional consequences can be significant. If their house has been broken into they may no longer feel safe living there, especially if they are elderly. Those who are elderly can be seen as 'easy targets' in street muggings. If an elderly person falls to the ground in these circumstances, this could easily lead to broken bones. Young people and those who live in areas of urban deprivation are more likely to experience crime. The death of Emily (see below) illustrates the tragic consequences of being a victim of crime.

Student commits suicide after assaults from boyfriend

In 2017 Angus Milligan, a student at Aberdeen University, was found guilty of eight charges of assaults on his girlfriend. Emily had not told her parents that she was being abused and sank into a deep depression. She was found dead in her halls of residence flat in March 2016. Her parents are devastated by her death.

Impact of crime on communities

High levels of crime may also damage community spirit, result in less neighbourliness and mean that people want to 'keep themselves to themselves' for fear of harassment or becoming involved in arguments. Areas that suffer from high levels of crime often suffer from vandalism and graffiti. This makes the area less desirable. Elderly people may be too afraid to go out in the evening.

Some crimes can rally a community together as illustrated in Blantyre. Reamonn Gormley, a student, was stabbed to death by two local youths. Thousands of people from communities around Blantyre marched against the use of knives and in support of the murdered teenager's family.

Impact of crime on society

- Businesses are affected by the cost of theft through crimes such as shoplifting. It is estimated that retail crime costs the sector over £1.6 billion per year.
- Violent crime costs the UK economy more than £124 billion a year, equivalent to £4700 for every household.
- Identity theft costs the UK over £2.7 billion a year.
- According to the Scottish Government, about £2.6 billion was budgeted for criminal justice in 2015/16.

Scottish criminal justice system

Scotland retained its own legal system after the Act of Union in 1707 and Scots law is still the legal system in Scotland today. Most law and order issues have been devolved to the Scottish Parliament (terrorism is one of the exceptions), and new laws are continually being passed. The Scottish Government has, for example, lowered the drink-driving limit.

Crown Office and Procurator Fiscal Service (COPFS)

In Scotland it is the Crown Office and Procurator Fiscal Service that decide whether or not to charge and prosecute individual(s). It is responsible for prosecuting crime and investigating complaints against the police. In an average year it handles almost 300,000 reports on offences committed.

The structures and powers of the court system

The three main courts dealing with criminal matters are:

- Justice of the Peace Courts
- the Sheriff Courts
- the High Court (of Justiciary).

Justice of the Peace Courts

A Justice of the Peace Court is a lay court, where the Justice of the Peace (JP) is supported by a legally qualified clerk. The court deals with less serious cases, such as theft, being drunk and disorderly, and traffic offences. The maximum sentence that a JP may impose is 60 days' imprisonment or a fine not exceeding £2500.

The Sheriff Court

A sheriff, who is an experienced solicitor or advocate, presides over trials at a Sheriff Court. The majority of both criminal and civil cases in Scotland are dealt with in a Sheriff Court.

- For solemn cases, a jury sits and the maximum sentence available is five years' imprisonment and/or an unlimited fine.
- For summary cases, the sheriff decides whether the accused is innocent or guilty and the maximum sentence is twelve months' imprisonment and/or a fine up to £10,000 (or pass to the High Court).

The High Court

The High Court is the supreme criminal court in Scotland and deals with the most serious of crimes. A jury of fifteen members of the public sits at the High Court. The custodial sentencing powers of the High Court are unlimited and for crimes such as murder, statute dictates that life imprisonment be imposed on the accused. The High Court also deals with all criminal appeal cases.

Court of Session

The Court of Session is Scotland's supreme civil court. It sits in Edinburgh and is both a trial court and a court of appeal. While most civil cases take place at Sheriff Courts, high-profile cases involving large companies or sizeable sums of money will be heard at the Court of Session. For example, much of the legal wrangling centring on Rangers Football Club was heard at the Court of Session.

UK Supreme Court

The creation of the UK Supreme Court in 2009 has led to accusations that it is undermining the independence and distinctiveness of the Scottish legal system. The Supreme Court can judge Scottish appeals if the accused is appealing under European Court of Human Rights (ECHR) legislation.

Verdicts in Scottish courts

There are three verdicts that a jury can arrive at in the Scottish criminal courts:

- **Guilty** There is a wide range of sentencing options such as prison or community service.
- **Not guilty** The accused is found innocent and until recently could not be prosecuted again on that charge. However, following on from changes in England, a new Double Jeopardy (Scotland) Act 2011 now allows a second trial if new compelling evidence emerges.
- **Not proven** This verdict is unique to Scotland. The accused is free to go but with the implication that they have escaped conviction *only* because of some doubt or lack of evidence. In 2012 MSP Michael McMahon launched a consultation into the 'not proven' verdict as he believes the verdict is 'illogical, inconsistent and confusing'.

Custodial and non-custodial sentences

A custodial sentence is when the guilty person is locked up for a set period of time. It could be to serve time either in a prison or Young Offender Institution (YOI). A non-custodial sentence covers a range of measure from fines to electronic tagging. (See page 64.)

The Children's Hearings System

The Children's Hearings System is based on the view that children who commit offences, and children who need care and protection, are dealt with in the same system – as these are often the same children. The Hearings System aims to ensure that the best interests of the child are met and that they receive the most appropriate intervention and support.

Who attends the Children's Hearing?

- The child or young person.
- The people who care for the child.
- The children's reporter – the person who decides if a child needs to be referred to a Children's Hearing. Children and young people are referred to the reporter from a number of sources, including the police, social workers, education and health professionals. They are referred because some aspect of their life is giving cause for concern.
- Three panel members who listen to the child's circumstances and then decide what measures are required.

What decisions can be made at a Hearing?

Various decisions can be made:

- The child should remain at home with support from other agencies, such as social work.
- The Hearing should continue at a later date – if more information is required.
- Compulsory Supervision Orders (CSOs) are made if panel members are worried about a young person. The Social Work Department or Local Authority must be involved in the young person's life and are responsible for looking after and helping the child. Most children on CSOs remain at home but if the panel members are worried about the safety of the child they might decide that the child should stay elsewhere. This can range from staying with other relatives or foster parents to care in a residential establishment.

Age of criminal responsibility may be raised to twelve

While children under the age of twelve cannot be prosecuted in court in Scotland, those aged eight and over can be referred to the Children's Hearings System for offending.

The Scottish Government has accepted a recommendation that the age of criminal responsibility be raised to twelve (it is ten in England and Wales). Child offenders will no longer have a criminal record and will be regarded as 'victims' rather than offenders. This is in line with the child-centred approach of the Children's Hearings System and in most cases it will be acknowledged that harmful deeds are caused by 'unmet needs' and can be referred on care and protection grounds. However, incidents involving children under twelve would still be investigated by the police.

Government responses to crime

Police

The main role of the police is to:

- protect the public (the traditional view of 'citizens in uniform')
- ensure law and order is kept in society
- detect criminals
- prevent crime.

Police Scotland

- Police Scotland came into being in April 2013 and is the second largest force in the UK after the Metropolitan Police. (England has retained its 43 police forces.)
- It is a merger of the eight Scottish police forces and the Scottish Crime and Drug Enforcement Agency.
- There are fourteen local policing divisions, each headed by a Local Police Commander who ensures that local policing in each area is responsive, accountable and tailored to meet local needs.
- The Police Scotland budget in 2014/15 was £1.06 billion and had a shortfall of £47 million despite a range of budget cuts.
- Police Scotland is led by Chief Constable Phil Gormley – he replaced Sir Stephen House, former Chief Constable of Strathclyde Police.
- There are 17,234 police officers in Scotland and 6701 police support staff. Unlike England, there has not been a reduction in police numbers. However, there has been a significant reduction in police civilian support staff.
- Police Scotland is encouraging greater diversity within the force – only 1% of officers are from an ethnic minority background (see 'Reversal of police ban on wearing headscarves while on duty', below).

Reversal of police ban on wearing headscarves while on duty

One attempt to encourage more police officers from an ethnic minority background was the decision in 2017 to allow police officers – special or regular – to wear a hijab. Chief Constable Phil Gormley wishes to improve diversity within police ranks – only 1% of officers come from an ethnic minority background compared to 4% of the population as a whole, rising to 12% in Glasgow. *The Herald* reported that a mother and daughter, Shafqat and Aleena Rafi, were set to become the first officers in Scotland to wear the hijab once they completed the recruitment process.

Crime prevention

Preventing crime before it happens is effective policing. For example, the Violence Reduction Unit (VRU) helps to reduce violent crime in Scotland. The VRU enlists police paramedics, former offenders and relatives of those killed in gang violence to speak to young people and make them aware of the devastation caused by knife crime. The success of the VRU is reflected in the following key statistics:

- The number of murders has fallen by 52% from 119 to 57 from 2006/07 to 2015/16.
- There has been a significant drop in knife violence and gang crime, as reflected in the reduction of violent crime.

> 'Overall crime has fallen to its lowest level in more than 40 years, violent crime is down 55%, the homicide rate has halved and handling of offensive weapons, including knife crime, is down by two-thirds.'
>
> (Michael Matheson, Justice Secretary (2016))

Knife crime prevention

- In 2012, the Scottish Government increased the maximum sentence for those found carrying a knife from four years to five years.
- Campaigns such as 'No Knives, Better Lives' educate young people about the dangers of carrying a knife and the devastating personal consequences it can have on their future.
- Wide use of stop and search by police discourages young people from carrying knives. However, this policy has been criticised. In June 2014 Police Scotland stated that routine stop and searches of young people would now end. All police officers have been retrained in new procedures.
- Crimes of handling an offensive weapon have dropped dramatically in Scotland, falling by almost 64% from 2007/08 to 2016/17.

Community policing

Working with the community reflects the view that policing is a partnership with local citizens. This should help the public to feel safer and to have greater confidence in the police, leading to a drop in crime. However, the revelation in 2014 that police are regularly carrying handguns while on patrol has been criticised by some MSPs. They argue that this weakens community policing and is a step towards the militarisation of the police. This view is reinforced by the increase in police use of taser guns (see below).

Death of former Aston Villa player after being tasered by police

Dalian Akinson, age 48, has died after being shot with a taser by police at his father's home. He suffered a cardiac arrest and died on his way to hospital. The president of the National Black Police Association expressed concern about the disproportionate use of tasers against ethnic minorities, who are three times more likely to have the weapons used on them by officers.

How effective is Police Scotland in tackling crime?

Police Scotland is effective as it eliminates duplication of services and in times of significant budget cuts makes the police more efficient. One centralised police force provides a more equal police service across Scotland and the centralisation of services such as the VRU and terrorism detection prevents and reduces crime. The number of officers attached to terrorist threats has been increased from 241 to 365. We still have a record number of police officers and crime has fallen with violent crime down 55%.

Scottish government official

> Police Scotland has been ineffective in improving the effectiveness of the service. Police stations have been closed and the new system fails to meet local needs. Yes, police numbers have remained the same, but the massive cuts to civilian staff have been a disaster. Regional call services have been closed and police officers have been forced to do civilian work. This explains the massive blunder when a police call centre failed to respond to an M9 car crash for three days.

Retired police officer

The penal system

Figure 7.3 highlights that the action taken against those who commit crimes is not simply to punish but to deter and rehabilitate the criminal thus reducing reoffending in the future. Many now question the effectiveness of a prison sentence for less serious crime and argue that alternatives to prison are more effective.

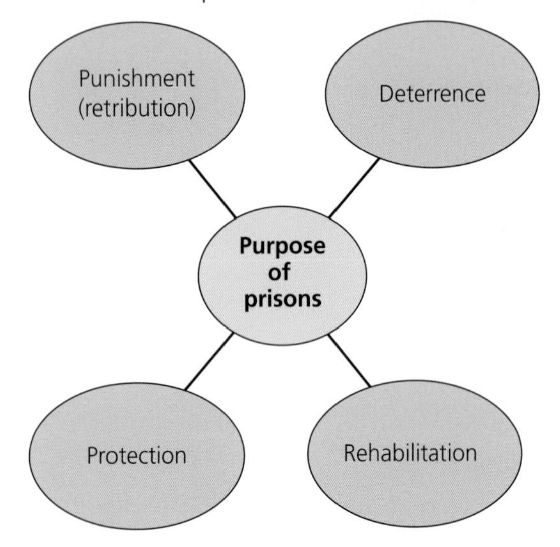

Figure 7.3 The purpose of prisons

Prisons work	Prisons fail
The public expects crime to be punished, and for violent crime, including murder, prison is the only option.	Short-term sentences do not work – more than half of those sentenced to jail terms of six months or less were reconvicted within a year.
If offenders are in jail then they cannot commit crime and so the public is protected.	Overcrowding in prison limits the number of prisoners who can take part in educational and offending behaviour programmes because there is no space for them.
A jail sentence deprives the offender of their liberty. The victims of crime then feel that justice has been done.	Overcrowding can create violent and chaotic conditions and makes it difficult for prison officers to control the abuse of drugs in jails and acts of violence between prisoners.
The possibility of a prison sentence will deter the individual from committing crime.	Around 70% of prisoners have histories of poor mental health and/or drug problems.
Prisons provide rehabilitation and offer an opportunity for the prisoner to receive treatment if they have drug or mental health issues.	In 2009 the number of Scottish prisoners passed 8000 for the first time. The figure today is about 7500.

Table 7.1 Do prisons work?

Scottish female prison statistics

- Over the past 20 years, women have gone from being 3.5% of the prison population to 5.7%.
- In March 2017, 333 women were behind bars (from 383 in 2015).
- 80% of women in Cornton Vale Women's Prison have mental health issues.
- Women are ten times more likely to self-harm than male prisoners.
- 71% of women in Corton Vale have used drugs before being sent to prison.
- 71% of women in prison have no qualifications, compared to 15% of the general public.
- Since 2008, 32 babies have been born while their mothers were in Cornton Vale.
- Some 16,500 children each year in Scotland are directly affected by parental imprisonment. Fifty per cent of looked-after children go on to receive custodial sentences.
- A separate 80-capacity prison is to be built to accommodate the most dangerous women prisoners. The remaining prisoners will be placed in new regional units which are designed to prepare female prisoners for release. Each will have a mother-and-child area and children will be able to stay overnight.

Country	Incarceration rate per 100,000
Scotland	143
England	144
Iceland	45
France	99
Netherlands	61

Table 7.2 Incarceration rates

Coping with the elderly

A 2017 report entitled 'Who Cares?' by HM Inspectorate of Prisons for Scotland highlights the dramatic increase in the numbers of prisoners over the age of 60 – an increase of one-fifth to 340 in just over a year. This increase is explained by a combination of an ageing population, longer sentences and an increased number of historic sex offenders being sent to prison. The report also highlights problems with accommodation in buildings which were never designed for so many older prisoners. Prisons find it difficult to meet the social and health needs of a frail elderly prison population. A report by the Scottish Parliament's Health and Sports Committee found that 236 prisoners had 'high' care needs such as mobility problems, dementia, incontinence and difficulty feeding themselves. It recommended that fellow prisoners should receive training to work as 'disability helpers' and also be given the opportunity to achieve college diplomas in health and social care.

Arguments for	Arguments against
The reoffending rate is lower for those given a non-custodial sentence and they are less expensive than a prison sentence.	The public and media perception is they are a soft option and fail to punish the prisoner.
They allow offenders to remain with family and possibly prevent the break-up of the family and children being put into care.	Many offenders break the curfew of Home Detention Curfews, and commit crimes. The private companies that run the service overcharge.
They enable offenders to contribute to community projects.	It is time-consuming and costly for offenders to be taken before the courts for failure to comply with a Community Payback Order (CPO).
Offenders avoid the stigma of imprisonment and the possibility of falling into bad company in prison.	They can be difficult to enforce and monitor. A significant number of offenders fail to complete their community service.
Prisons remain a 'revolving door' with 43% of women reconvicted within a year of leaving prison – for men the figure is 35%. Women fare worse than men after prison. Women do better on alternative measures – around 95% complete community-service sentences, compared to only 75% of men.	

Table 7.3 Arguments for and against non-custodial sentences

Main alternatives to prison

Community Payback Orders

A court can order between 20 and 300 hours of supervised work which must be completed within six months of the date of sentence. The offender can carry out their sentence in their free time if they are in full- or part-time work. The offender is also encouraged to tackle any addiction issues.

Electronic monitoring or tagging

This is used to enforce the Home Detention Curfew (HDC) since its introduction in 2006. The service is run by the private sector. In Scotland, the security service is provided by G4S and the contract is worth £13 million over five years.

Fines and compensation orders

The two main types of financial penalty are fines, and compensation to the victim.

Questions and model answers

Remember

Knowledge and understanding questions will have 4, 6 or 8 marks allocated and you will need to answer three questions.

Remember

In a describe question, up to 3 marks can be awarded for each description you make, depending on its quality, level of detail, relevance, accuracy and exemplification.

Describe question

The Children's Hearings System can help young people in Scotland in different ways.

Describe, **in detail**, **two** ways that the Children's Hearings System can help young people in Scotland. **6 marks**

Model answer

The Children's Hearings System helps young people by providing a relaxed atmosphere where young people can discuss their offending behaviour. It is less intimidating than going to an adult court and they will get help and support from school, social workers and the police to change their behaviour. It provides support not punishment.

The Children's Hearings System helps young people who perhaps have been neglected by parents who have a drink and drugs problem. The young person can be placed in a safe place, perhaps with other relatives or with foster parents, and be supported by social workers.

Marker's comment

This is a very good answer because it is relevant and detailed. The candidate covers two factors. The first paragraph would receive 3 marks because it accurately identifies the support given to a young offender. This is developed by detailed reference to the nature of support available.

The second paragraph would also easily get 3 marks because it accurately identifies the support given to a child at risk. This is developed with excellent exemplification.

Overall a high-quality answer deserving full marks. **6 marks**

Hints & tips

Always structure your answers in paragraphs. Avoid list-type answers or bullet points.

Make sure you take account of how many marks a question is worth. You should base the length of your answers on the time you should allocate to 4-mark, 6-mark or 8-mark questions.

Explain question

Other punishments are increasingly being used as alternatives to prison sentences in the UK.

Explain, **in detail**, **two** reasons why other punishments are increasingly being used as alternatives to prison sentences in the UK. **6 marks**

Model answer

With the massive cuts to prison budgets, there are fewer staff and less money to run effective rehabilitation programmes. This means that some offenders are released with the same addictions or issues they had when they went into prison. Many reoffend and return to prison.

Alternatives to prison such as electronic tagging and community service orders reduce the risk of reoffending. The individual can still keep their job and if they do community service they are improving the community. They might paint a children's playground and this might give them back some self-esteem and make them less likely to commit another crime.

Marker's comment

This is a very good answer because it is relevant and detailed. The first paragraph would get 3 marks because it accurately identifies the problems facing prisons in terms of rehabilitation. Furthermore, there is a level of analysis in commenting that 'This means ...'.

The second paragraph would easily achieve 3 marks because it accurately identifies two alternatives. This is developed and exemplified with relevant detail by mentioning keeping a job and improved self-esteem.

Overall a high-quality answer easily deserving of full marks. **6 marks**

Remember

For a 6-mark answer you must cover at least two factors in depth. In an explain question, a maximum of 4 marks can be given for each detailed point you give, depending on its quality, level of detail, relevance, accuracy and exemplification. In your answer, it is also good to show the interaction of various factors.

Part Four: International Issues

This section of the book provides summary course notes for the International Issues Section of the course.

You will have studied one of the following topics as part of your National 5 International Issues Section:

- World Powers, or
- World Issues.

The major World Power studied must be drawn from one of the G7 countries (excluding the UK) or one of the following: Brazil, China, India, Russia, South Africa.

In the World Issues section of the International Issues Section you will have studied the cause, consequences and attempts at resolution of a particular world issue. We will cover two World Issues in this book: development issues in Africa, and international terrorism.

In the knowledge section of the exam you will answer **three questions** on this Section and these questions will be allocated 4, 6 or 8 marks each.

Chapter 8
World Powers: The United States of America

What you should know 

To be successful in this section, you should be able to **know** and **understand**:

* the American political system:
  * the constitutional arrangements and the main institutions of government at federal and state level
  * the participation and representation of the American people in decision-making
* the impact of the following social and economic issues:
  * employment
  * poverty/inequality
  * population movement
  * health
  * education
  * crime and law
* the influence of the USA on other countries:
  * political influence
  * economic influence
  * military influence.

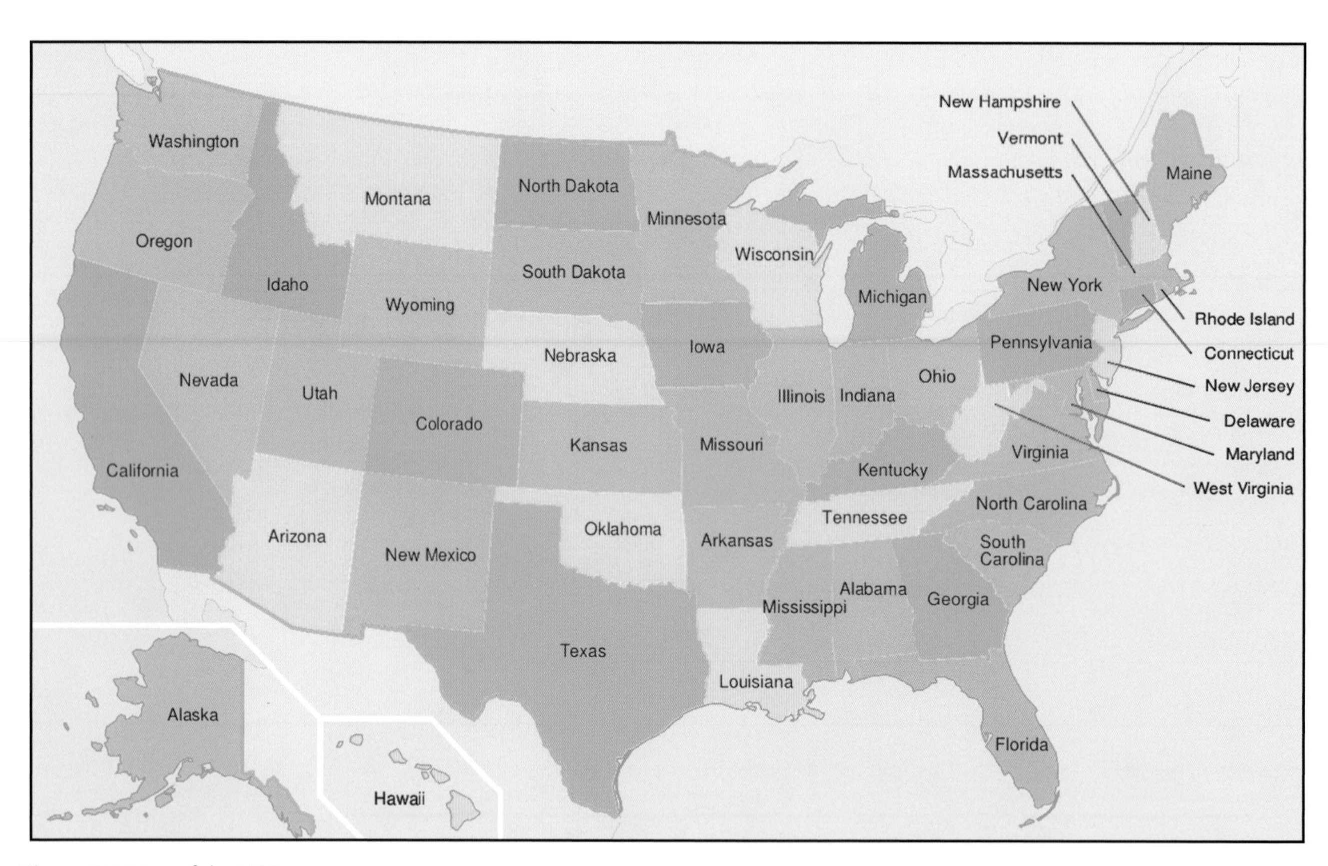

Figure 8.1 Map of the USA

Background

The USA is the third largest country in the world in area and its population of 325 million makes it the third most populous country in the world behind China and India.

The population consists of five main ethnic groups as shown in Figure 8.2.

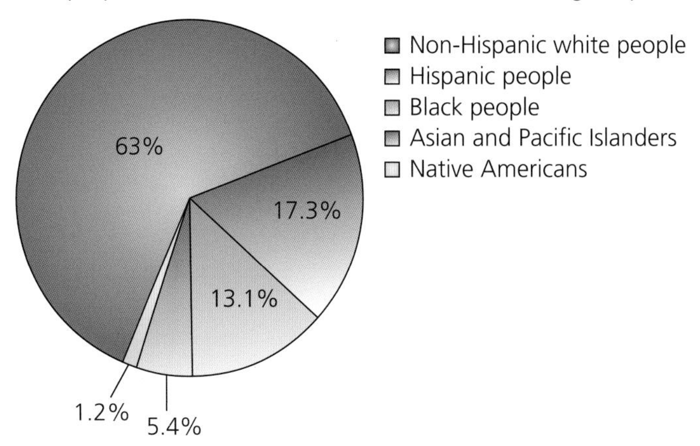

Figure 8.2 Ethnic groups in the USA

The USA is the home of capitalism and it has the largest economy in the world, valued at $16,768 billion. (China has the second highest valued at $9240 billion.)

The American political system

The USA has a federal system of government with power divided between the central federal government and the 50 states, such as California (see Table 8.1). All powers not assigned by the Constitution to the federal government are reserved to the states.

State powers	Federal powers
Local laws, e.g. age of compulsory education, authority over armed forces and age of consent to marry	The armed forces and post office
Punishment, e.g. the use and forms of capital punishment and state prisons	Overseeing federal prisons
Provision of roads, and schools	Overseeing foreign and interstate trade
Management of public health and safety	Conducting foreign relations including declaring war and the negotiations of peace
Overseeing trade within the state, including local taxation	The economy of the USA

Table 8.1 State and federal powers in the USA

The US Constitution

This document, written in the eighteenth century, outlines the **separation of powers** and includes 27 amendments, the first ten of which are referred to as the Bill of Rights.

Key words

Separation of powers: To prevent any one branch of government becoming too powerful, and to ensure cooperation, the Constitution outlines how powers are separated between Congress, the president and Supreme Court.

Amendment 1 guarantees freedom of speech.

Amendment 2 gives Americans the right to carry guns.

Table 8.2 outlines the separation of power between the three branches of government. This division applies not just to the federal structure but also to the states.

Each state has its own Governor and state legislatures elected by the people and its own judicial system.

Branch	Body	Duties
Executive	President and cabinet	To propose policies and run the country
Legislative	Congress (Senate and House of Representatives)	To pass, reject or amend laws
Judicial	Nine judges of the Supreme Court	To interpret laws

Table 8.2 The three federal branches of government

Checks and balances

Powers	Limitations
President is Commander-in-Chief of the armed forces, responsible for foreign affairs and also head of state.	Only Congress has the power to ratify laws.
President appoints Supreme Court judges.	Senate has to approve appointments to the Supreme Court and president cannot remove a judge.
President can veto (reject) a law passed by Congress.	Congress can overturn a veto by a two-thirds majority.
President can by-pass Congress by using an Executive Order.	Courts can study an Executive Order and decide if it is legal.
President can propose laws to Congress.	Only Congress can pass laws – President Obama's gun control bill was rejected by Congress.

Table 8.3 Role of the president: powers and limitations

Participation and representation

In the USA the people can participate in electing representatives at local, state and national level. A single elector can vote for up to 30 officials and representatives in one election.

Local	State	Federal
At county level, electors may be asked to vote for the sheriff, a tax collector, the mayor, a dog catcher and numerous other posts.	Every two years electors choose representatives for state posts including state legislature, and every four years for the state governor.	At national level, electors can vote every two years for their representative in the State Assembly, every four years for their presidential candidate and every six years for their senator.

Table 8.4 Political representatives in the USA

Ballot propositions

While electors choose their representative, they can also take part in decision-making in their state by voting yes or no to various propositions. This is equivalent to UK referendums.

November 2016 USA elections – ballot propositions

In November 2016, 34 states offered a combined total of 157 propositions to their respective citizens. California alone had 17 propositions. The propositions included the following:

- Florida – Marijuana should be legalised for medical use.
- California – Marijuana should be legalised for medical or recreational use.
- Maine – The state minimum wage should be increased to $12.

Electing the president

The president of the USA is not chosen directly by the US people. Instead, presidents are elected by 'electors' who are chosen by popular vote on a state-by-state basis. These 'electors' then award their states' electoral college votes to the candidate with the greatest support in their state. Overall, in the 2016 election, the Republican candidate Donald Trump won 306 of the electoral college votes, compared to 232 for the Democratic candidate Hilary Clinton and so became president.

Yet Hilary Clinton won the most popular votes (the total number of votes each candidate received across the country). Clinton received 65.5 million votes compared to 62.8 million votes for Trump.

Figure 8.3 Donald Trump

Party	Popular vote 2016	Popular vote 2012
Democrats	48.1	51.0
Republican	46.2	47.1
	Electoral college vote 2016	**Electoral college vote 2012**
Democrats	43.2	61.7
Republican	56.8	38.3

Table 8.4 US presidential election results 2012 and 2016 (%)

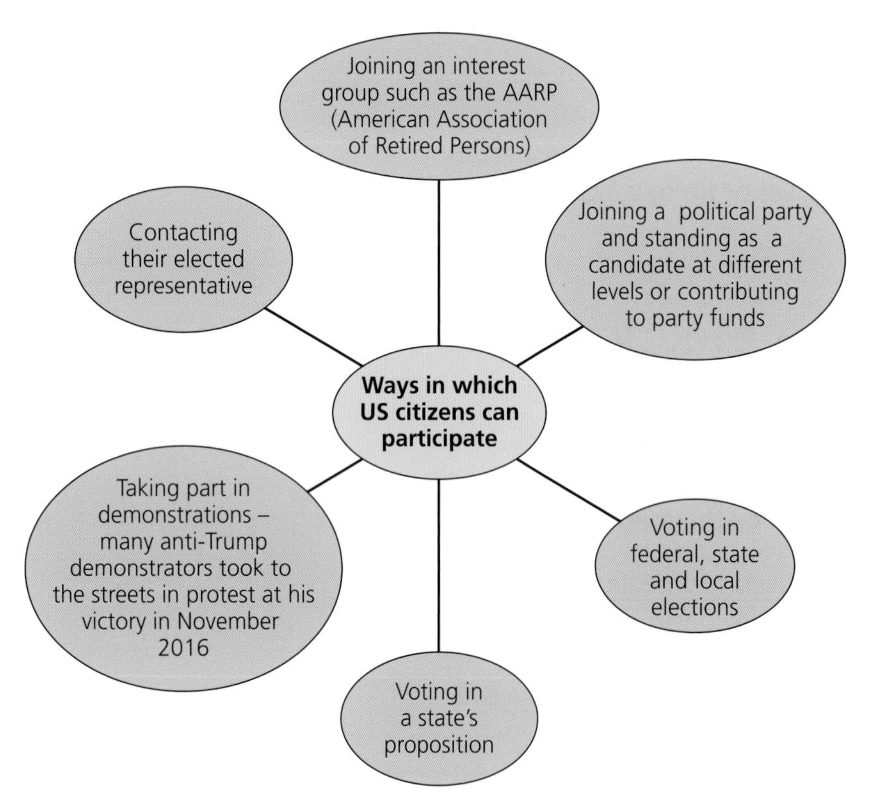

Figure 8.4 Ways in which US citizens can participate

Why do some people and groups not vote?

- Registering to vote can be complicated, and some Republican-controlled states pass electoral procedures that discourage ethnic minorities from voting.
- Some feel that voting is a waste of time as it will not improve their life in the **ghetto**.
- Some feel that there are too many elections in the USA and that the ballot paper is long and complicated.
- Many Hispanic people are illegal immigrants and do not qualify to vote.

Key words

Ghetto: A run-down inner-city area with high crime.

The impact of Obama on ethnic minority participation

Obama's run for presidency in 2008 energised ethnic minority turnout as it opened up the possibility of the election of the first black president. Voting turnout in the 2008 presidential election was just under 63%, the highest since the 1960s. A staggering 95% of the black electorate voted for Obama and 71% of Hispanic people also voted for him. Obama repeated his 2008 victory in 2012.

Political representation

Women and ethnic minorities are under-represented in Congress. However, there has been a modest improvement in the diversity of politicians elected in November 2016 as outlined below:

- Women membership remains the same at 104 (a lowly 19%) with an increase of 1 in the Senate to 21 and a reduction of 1 in the House of Representatives.
- Afro-American membership has increased from 46 to 49 in the House of Representatives, and there is the highest ever representation in the Senate at 3.
- Hispanic membership has increased to a record 38, with 34 in the House of Representatives.
- Asian/Pacific Islander American membership has increased to 18, with 3 serving in the Senate.

Rights and responsibilities

The USA is a democratic country. All citizens are given rights and privileges, but with these rights come responsibilities.

Rights	Responsibilities
The right to free speech, a free press and freedom of religion	To respect the rights, beliefs and opinions of others
The right to vote	To register to use your vote
The right to a fair, speedy trial by a jury of your peers	To respect and obey state and federal laws
The right to protest and assembly	To protest in a legal way

Table 8.5 Rights and responsibilities of American citizens

Social and economic issues

Employment and inequality: causes and impact

The USA is one of the most unequal societies in the world with a vast inequality of wealth between the rich and poor. This economic inequality creates massive social inequalities in education, housing and health provision. The poverty trap, the recent economic recession, racial discrimination and language barriers are some of the main causes of inequality and explain why for most poor people, the **American Dream** only happens when they sleep.

Key words

American Dream: The belief that through hard work any American can be a success.

- 15% of Americans (around 47 million) live below the poverty line, with 12 million in low paid employment. One in five children live in poverty.
- About 25% of black families live in poverty compared to 40% in the mid-1960s.
- In 2015 President Obama highlighted racial inequality – the median white household had net assets of $142,000; the median black one had $11,000. The housing collapse of 2009 onwards had a far greater impact on black people.
- The economic crisis of 2008 increased the nation's debt and forced the Government to reduce public spending. The austerity cuts have had most impact on the poor.
- Most of the low-skill, high-wage jobs in manufacturing no longer exist and students who fail to graduate from high school often find themselves trapped in low-paid employment.
- Deteriorating family structures among the poor contribute to the cycle of poverty – most poor children live in single-parent homes.

Government policies

- The American Recovery and Reinvestment Act of 2009 (ARRA) was introduced in response to the massive economic crisis of 2008 with the aim of helping those hardest hit by the recession. It tried to boost employment and economic recovery with a massive programme of government expenditure. While this increased the budget deficit, it did provide employment for millions and improve housing stock and educational opportunities.
- President Obama resisted demands from Republicans to reduce welfare payments. However, President Trump wishes to cut federal programmes that help the poor.
- Households with low incomes can claim a $1000 credit against their federal income taxes for every dependent child. This means that many poor families pay no income tax.
- The most important tax-based cash-transfer programme is the Earned Income Tax Credit (EITC). This aims to encourage the poor to join the

labour force. A married couple with three or more children can receive $5000 or more.

- In 2013, $60 million was paid out through the EITC and $24 million through child tax credits.
- Federal government spending on food stamps has more than doubled between 2008 and 2016.
- The Temporary Assistance for Needy Families (TANF) supplements support for needy families. Payments are conditional on the recipient trying to find work and are only available for a five-year period. Prior to the 2008 recession, the number of claimants had halved as work was plentiful. The numbers have now increased from 12 million in 2007 to 15 million in 2017.

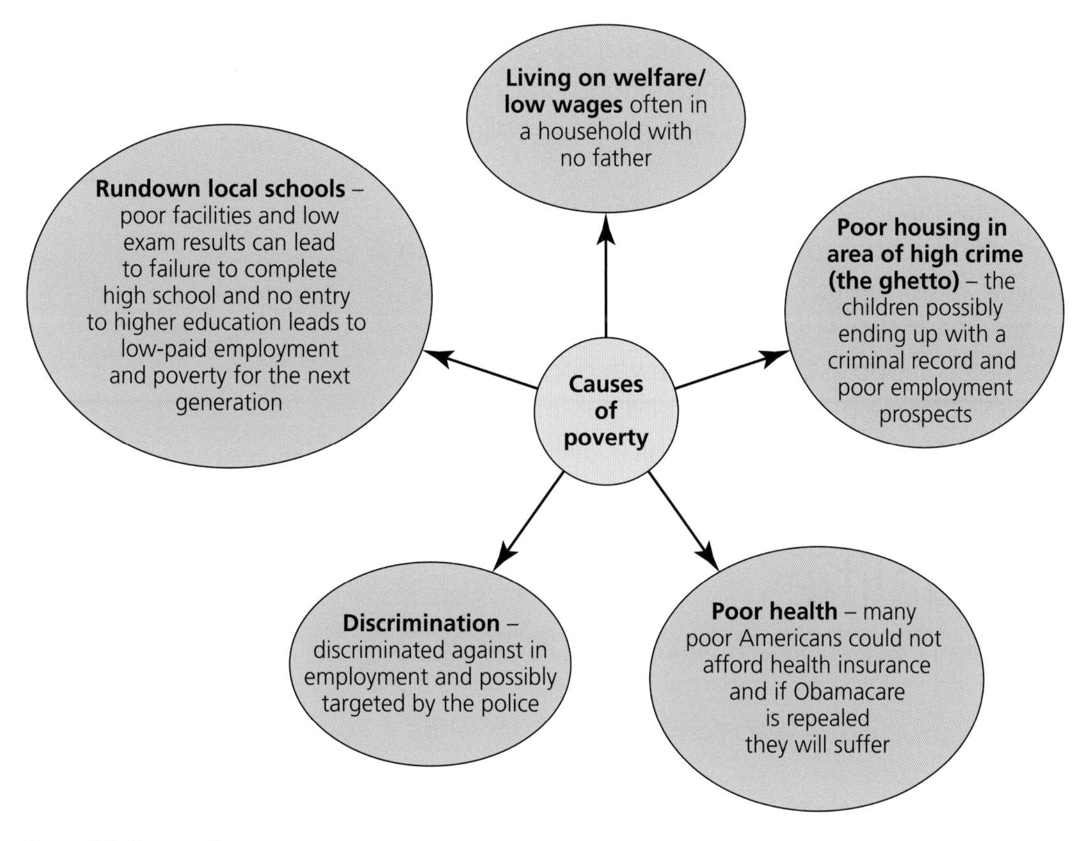

Figure 8.5 Causes of poverty

Impact of education inequalities

- At the age of nine, 86% of black and 82% of Hispanic boys cannot read proficiently.
- 36% of white people have a bachelor's degree compared to 21% of black people.

Asian-Americans

An ethnic-minority success story is that of the achievements of Asian-Americans – 49% of Asian-Americans have a bachelor's degree compared with 28% of the general population. In 2014, 41% of Berkeley University's enrolment were Asian-Americans.

However, Asians feel that affirmative action discriminates against them at the top universities as black people and Hispanic people are admitted with lower scores. The view of the courts is that universities may take race into consideration, but racial quotas are not permissible.

Government action

- As part of ARRA, $53 billion was allocated to improve state schooling in poorer areas and extra funding was given to the Head Start Program which provides free school meals to schools in poorer areas. $30 billion was given to support students from poor families attending college.
- The Race to the Top Fund aims to reduce educational inequalities by reducing expulsion and dropout rates of ethnic minority students, improving exam results in inner-city schools and increasing college admissions of ethnic minorities.
- The Opportunity Scholarship Program, which is subsidised by the federal Government, offers school vouchers based on a lottery system to 2000 children a year. Worth up to $12,000, each scholarship covers the cost of tuition fees in a private school.
- The Trump administration supports the rapid growth of charter schools, fee-free schools that are publicly subsidised but independently run. It also supports a school-voucher scheme which gives public funds to pay for places at private schools.

Health inequalities

- Black babies are more than twice as likely as white babies to die before their first birthday.
- Life expectancy for black people is 74 years compared to 79 for white people.
- Prior to the introduction of the Affordable Care Act, 13% of Americans did not have health insurance.

Government policies

- The Affordable Care Act (Obamacare) came into force in 2013 and aims to ensure that all Americans have health insurance. The federal government and states subsidise the health payments of those on a low income. The result is that 9 million more Americans now have insurance. The Act is unpopular with richer Americans who now pay far more for their health insurance.
- Donald Trump promised to abolish Obamacare if he became president. Congress failed to pass such a bill in July 2017. However, it is clear that changes will eventually be made to the provision of healthcare in America.

Crime and the law – is there racial discrimination?

- Black people and Hispanic people are imprisoned at twice the rate of white people.
- A third of young black people end up in prison. Black people also receive longer sentences than their white counterparts.
- 40% of the current death-row population is black.
- Over the last five years there have been numerous cases of black people being killed by police officers. In Ferguson in 2013 there were widespread riots when a white officer was acquitted of shooting an unarmed black teenager, Michael Brown.

Government response

- All police officers are now required to record incidents with the public to provide evidence if needed.
- One cause of tension is the availability of inexpensive guns. Obama made it his priority to reduce gun violence and protect communities, especially from mass shootings. He proposed tighter background checks and the banning of military assault weapons. The Republican-controlled Congress ensured, however, that no reforms took place during his presidency.

Political discrimination?

Asian-Americans are under-represented in political office. Although they make up 5.4% of the population, only 3.3% of Congress representatives were Asian-Americans in 2017.

Federal Voting Rights Act

In 2013 the Supreme Court ruled that states should be allowed to introduce their own electoral laws. Southern states have introduced more stringent electoral procedures which discourage black voting. In Texas, new identity requirements would have prevented 600,000 black people from voting. This was declared unconstitutional by the courts and Texas was forced to drop these new requirements.

Population movement

The USA is the land of opportunity and is described as a nation of immigrants. However, the increase in the number of illegal immigrants has made this a political issue.

Recent policies on immigration

- Between 2009 and 2015 the Obama administration deported an average of about 360,000 people a year.
- President Obama tried to reform immigration during his eight-year presidency but failed because of Republican opposition in Congress.

- In 2013 Obama used an Executive Order to grant amnesty to about 4 million of the estimated 12 million immigrants who would meet the terms of the Order.
- President Trump wants to deport all illegal immigrants with criminal records. However, deportation hearings can take years to complete in the immigration court.
- Trump supports a wall being built along the USA/Mexico border. This divides Americans along party lines – only 8% of Democrats support a new border wall compared with 74% of Republicans.

Arguments for immigration	Arguments against immigration
Most immigrants pay taxes and contribute to society – California has 3 million undocumented immigrants who contribute $130 billion of California's gross domestic product (GDP).	President Trump has stated that there are over 2 million illegal immigrants with criminal records threatening the security and wellbeing of US citizens. (The Migrant Policy Institute disagrees and places the figure at 820,000.)
Many immigrants work in undesirable jobs that most citizens would not wish to do – they are not stealing jobs.	President Trump believes that immigrants are a cause of unemployment. He has said, 'We are going to defend our workers, protect our jobs and finally put America first.'
The American population is ageing as is its workforce. Immigrants with their young families address this problem.	State governments have to provide social services for immigrants. Education, for example, costs $11,000 a year per child.
America benefits from the diversity of cultures and languages.	The non-Hispanic white population is continually declining and Republicans argue that their values are threatened.

Table 8.6 Arguments for and against immigration

Influence on other countries

The USA has been the dominant economic and military power across all continents of the world for 30 years. Its culture and products – from Coca Cola to McDonald's – circle the globe.

Political and military influence

- The UN headquarters are based in New York and the USA is a permanent member of the Security Council. In August 2017 America persuaded the Security Council to impose harsher sanctions on North Korea.
- The USA is the dominant nation in NATO and contributes the majority of the budget.
- The USA has a massive military presence and has troops and bases around the globe. Its aircraft carriers patrol the Asian seas to combat the new aggressive actions of China.
- However, President Trump with his slogan of 'America First' is redefining America's role as the 'world's policeman'.
- Since 9/11 (the attacks on the USA on 11 September 2001 by the Islamic terrorist group al-Qaeda), the USA has mobilised the international community in its 'war on terrorism'. Initial success in Iraq and Afghanistan has not brought peace and stability to the Middle East. ISIS and its off-shoots have created chaos in Syria and Iraq.
- America's military outlay accounts for 37% of global military spending. The USA spends four times more than China, the world's second highest spender, and dominates land, air, sea and space.

Economic influence

- The US economy as measured by gross domestic product (GDP) is by far the largest in the world, even as China steadily closes the gap (see Table 8.7).
- The American economy is the bedrock of the global financial system. Over 80% of all financial world transactions are in dollars.
- America is the world's number one producer of oil and natural gas.
- America spends more than any other country on foreign aid ($33 billion in 2015). This gives America political and economic clout around the world, buying goodwill and influence.

Social influence

- America's culture and products circle the globe. American companies, such as McDonald's, dominate the fast food industries around the world. American culture is universal as a result of its Hollywood films and television programmes.

Country	GDP ($ trillion)	As a percentage of the world's GDP
USA	18.0	24.3
China	11.0	14.8
Japan	4.3	5.9

Table 8.7 Top GDPs around the world

Questions and model answers

Describe question ?

Governments have made many attempts to tackle social and economic inequality.

Describe, **in detail**, **two** ways in which the government of the world power you have studied has tried to tackle social and economic inequality. **6 marks**

Model answer

Health inequalities are a major issue in America. President Obama brought in the Affordable Care Act. Many poor people could not afford or were denied private health insurance. Under the Act, 8 million more Americans now are covered by insurance. This has helped many ethnic minorities as they have the highest rates of poverty.

The government has also brought in measures to improve the academic performance of ethnic minority students and their employability. The Race to the Top Fund with a budget of $34 billion has helped to reduce expulsion and dropout rates of ethnic minority students and improved exam results in inner-city schools. This will hopefully increase college admission for these students.

⇨

Marker's comment

In this answer, two factors are described. The first paragraph would get 3 marks because it accurately identifies and develops a recent health policy with excellent exemplification.

The second paragraph would also receive 3 marks because it accurately identifies and develops a recent education policy with excellent exemplification.

Overall a very good and high-quality answer deserving of full marks.

6 marks

Explain question

World powers have the ability to influence other countries.

Explain, **in detail**, **two** reasons why the world power you have studied has the ability to influence other countries. **6 marks**

Model answer

One reason America is able to influence other countries is because of its military might which covers the globe. Its bases in Asia protect countries such as Taiwan from Chinese aggression. President Trump has warned North Korea to end its aggressive actions against its Asian neighbours.

A second reason is that America is the richest country in the world and its companies, such as McDonald's, span the globe. The American economy is at the centre of the global finance system with over 80% of all financial world transactions being in dollars. This highlights the economic influence of the USA.

Marker's comment

In this answer the first paragraph would get 3 marks because it identifies military strength as a reason and uses the protection of Taiwan as an example.

The second paragraph would also get 3 marks because it accurately identifies economic strength as a reason and uses the influence of American companies abroad as an example.

Overall a very good and high-quality answer deserving of full marks.

6 marks

Remember

Knowledge and understanding questions will have 4, 6 or 8 marks allocated and you will need to answer three questions.

Hints & tips

Always structure your answers in paragraphs. Avoid list-type answers or bullet points.

Remember

In a describe question, up to 3 marks can be awarded for each description you make, depending on their quality, level of detail, relevance, accuracy and exemplification.

Hints & tips

Make sure you take account of how many marks a question is worth. You should base the length of your answers on the time you should allocate to 4-mark, 6-mark or 8-mark questions.

Remember

For a 6-mark answer you must cover at least two factors in depth. In an explain question, a maximum of 4 marks can be given for each detailed point you give, depending on their quality, level of detail, relevance, accuracy and exemplification. In your answer, it is also good to show the interaction of various factors.

Chapter 9
World Powers: The Republic of South Africa

What you should know 

To be successful in this section, you should **know** and **understand**:

- the South African political system:
  - the constitutional arrangements and the main institutions of government at national and state level
  - the participation and representation of the South African people in decision-making
- the impact of the following social and economic issues:
  - employment
  - poverty/inequality
  - population movement
  - health
  - education
  - crime and law
- the influence of South Africa on other countries in the following spheres:
  - political influence
  - economic influence
  - military influence.

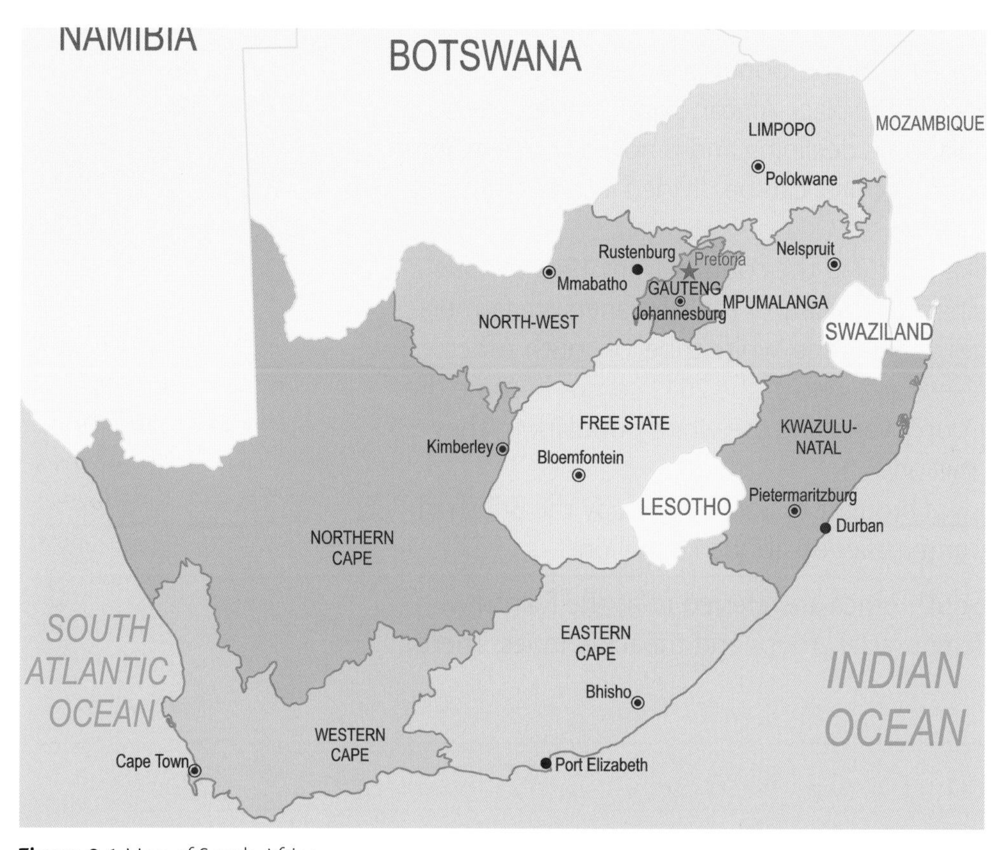

Figure 9.1 Map of South Africa

Background

- South Africa is the wealthiest country in Southern Africa. It is rich in natural resources and has a modern manufacturing industry.
- South Africa has a population of 56 million (based on 2017 mid-year estimates) with over 80% being black South Africans.
- South Africa is a multi-racial democracy with free elections based on a Proportional Representation (PR) electoral system.
- Only in 1994 were the black South Africans given the right to vote and full social and economic rights. Prior to this the white minority ruled the country under the **apartheid system**. Its **legacy** still impacts on the lives of all South Africans.

South Africa is one of the most unequal societies in the world. Wealth has been transferred from white people to black people but it has not been shared equally. A very wealthy black elite has been created, but the majority still face severe social and economic inequalities.

Key words

Legacy of apartheid: The social and economic inequalities that still exist today between the races as a result of white rule (1948–94) which discriminated against non-whites.

Archbishop Desmond Tutu stated in 1994:
'Apartheid has left a ghastly legacy. There is a horrendous housing shortage and high unemployment, health care is not easily affordable by the majority; Bantu (black African) education has left us with a massive educational crisis; there is gross maldistribution of wealth.'

Population

South Africa has a population of 56 million people, made up of the following racial groups:

- **Black Africans** make up 81% of the population, with the main tribal groups being Xhosa and Zulu. The black African population is increasing.
- **Whites**: The white population is declining and is now only 4.5 million (8% of the total population). Whites can be divided into two groups:
  - **English-speaking**
  - **Afrikaners**: The Afrikaners ruled the country from 1948 to 1994 under the policy of apartheid. Many of the Afrikaners are farmers and regard themselves as being the 'white tribe' of South Africa.
- **Coloureds**: Those of mixed race, who in the 2011 census became the second largest ethnic group, overtaking the white population. They now number almost 5 million.
- **Asian**: This population was brought to South Africa by the British in the nineteenth century and makes up about 1.4 million.

The 56 million citizens of South Africa are referred to as the Rainbow Nation because of the different racial groups and tribal identities. There are eleven official languages.

Political issues

South Africa is a successful and stable democracy with free elections at all levels of government based on the party list PR system. The written Constitution provides a wide range of rights to its citizens.

The rights of citizens are protected by the Constitutional Court, which is made up of senior judges, and which can also declare government actions illegal. Citizens can criticise government actions using the **free press**, and can freely join groups such as political parties, pressure groups or trade unions.

Key words

Free press: Media that is not restricted or censored by the government.

However, some critics have stated that South Africa is becoming a one-party state, referring to the dominance of the African National Congress (ANC) and the fact that some of its members participate in corrupt activities. The last two police chiefs have been sacked and one is in jail for corruption. President Zuma has been criticised for building a vast homestead that will cost South African citizens 328 million rand (over £23 million).

National government

Executive

The National Assembly elects the president from among its members. The president and the cabinet make up the government. The president leads the cabinet and is the executive head of state. The president may not serve more than two five-year terms in office. The president, deputy president and 25 ministers make up the cabinet. The deputy president and ministers are appointed by the president, who can also dismiss them. The current president is Jacob Zuma and he also appoints and can remove the premiers of the eight provinces controlled by the ANC.

Legislature

South Africa's Parliament consists of a national assembly (400 members) and the National Council of Provinces (NCOP). Elections for both houses are held every five years based on a system of PR.

Judiciary

South Africa has an independent judiciary who are guardians of the Constitution. The highest court is the **Constitutional Court**, which has eleven judges, including the chief justice. President Zuma has criticised the judges but it would weaken democracy if the courts were to be controlled by the ANC.

Key words

Constitutional Court: The highest court of the land and guardian of the Constitution.

Provincial government

All nine provinces in South Africa have their own legislature and government, which is led by a premier. Eight of the nine premiers were appointed by Jacob Zuma in 2014. Provincial governments implement national government policies.

Local government

There are 283 local councils, which are referred to as municipalities. However, large cities such as Cape Town and Johannesburg have their own metropolitan municipalities. Many mayors of these municipalities are failing to deliver basic services, partly because of mismanagement and corruption.

How can South African citizens participate in politics?

- By voting in national, provincial and local elections.
- By joining or standing as a candidate for a political party such as ANC or Democratic Alliance.
- By contacting (e.g. by telephone, letter, internet) their elected representatives.
- By joining a pressure group, such as the Treatment Action Group (TAC), which is demanding greater access to anti-AIDS drugs.
- By joining a trade union such as the National Union of Miners (NUM). However, many miners have lost faith in the union after the Marikana massacre of 2012 and have taken part in illegal action (see Figure 9.2).

Figure 9.2 On 16 August 2012, 34 striking miners were killed by police at a platinum mine near Marikana, South Africa

Political parties

African National Congress (ANC) 	The ANC dominates South African politics and is the party of Nelson Mandela and black liberation. It has won all five of the national elections but its support is declining. Many blacks have lost faith in the ANC.
Democratic Alliance (DA) 	This party replaced the NNP as the official opposition after the 2004 elections and has increased its support in every national election since. It gained control of the Western Cape after the 2009 elections. Its main supporters are whites, people of mixed race and Asians.
Inkatha Freedom Party (IFP)	The IFP, led by Chief Buthelezi, draws its support largely from Zulu-speaking South Africans and supports greater powers for the provincial governments. It is a party in decline and it lost heavily to the ANC in the 2014 elections in Kwazulu-Natal.
Economic Freedom Fighters (EFF) 	This was a new political party formed in 2013 by former ANC member Julius Malema. It supports a left-wing agenda. It came third in the 2014 elections but failed to win enough black support to challenge the ANC.

Table 9.1 South Africa's main political parties

Elections

National elections take place every five years under a PR system, which closely matches votes to seats won by a political party. It encourages the formation of new political parties, such as the EFF in 2013. This weakens the formation of a strong opposition as new parties divide and weaken the opposition to the ANC.

Party	2004		2009		2014	
	Seats	Votes (%)	Seats	Votes (%)	Seats	Votes (%)
ANC	279	69.9	264	65.9	249	62.1
Democratic Alliance	50	12.6	67	16.7	89	22.2
Inkatha Freedom Party	28	6.9	18	4.5	10	2.4
Economic Freedom Fighters	n/a	n/a	n/a	n/a	25	6.3

Table 9.2 National assembly election results for the main political parties, 2004–14

Hints & tips

In order to try to remember the names of the main political parties in South Africa you could use the following mnemonic (AND):

- ✓ *African National Congress*
- ✓ *Inkatha Freedom Party*
- ✓ *Democratic Alliance*

Mmusi Mamene – leader of the DA

This mainly white and coloured party appointed Mamene as their first black leader. Despite increasing their votes and seats in the 2014 general election, the DA only won 6% of the black vote. Mamene's aim is to increase black support and to end the view that the DA is a white party. In the 2016 local government election, the ANC experienced its worst ever electoral performance, winning only 54% of the votes. In contrast, the DA won its highest ever with 27%.

Figure 9.3 Mmusi Mamene

Rights and responsibilities

As South Africa is a democratic country, all citizens are given rights and privileges, but with these rights come responsibilities.

Rights	Responsibilities
The right to free speech, a free press and freedom of religion.	To respect the rights, beliefs and opinions of others.
The right to vote.	To register to use your vote.
The right to a fair, speedy trial by a jury of your peers.	To respect and obey national and provincial laws.
The right to equality and equal rights (Article 9.2 discriminates against whites).	For whites to accept that Article 9.2, which discriminates against whites, is fair.

Table 9.3 Rights and responsibilities of South African citizens

Is South Africa a successful democracy?

Arguments for

- South Africa is a stable model of democracy for Africa. There have been four peaceful elections based on PR. In the 2014 election, over 35 political parties participated, with 13 parties now sitting in the National Assembly.
- South Africa has a free press and a civil society that can criticise the Government and expose corruption.
- South Africa has a liberal Constitution guaranteeing freedom to its citizens. It provides for an independent judiciary. The Constitutional Court ordered Mbeki to provide drugs to combat AIDS. In 2017 the court defied President Zuma and declared that MPs could vote in a secret ballot in any motion to remove the president.

Arguments against

- There is a fear that South Africa is becoming a one-party state. The ANC has won all four post-apartheid elections convincingly and controls eight of the nine provinces. Only in Western Cape is it in opposition.
- There is an issue of corruption, with leading ANC members being sent to jail. President Zuma built a vast homestead that will cost the citizens 328 million rand.

- The policy of **Black Transformation** politics could threaten the independence of judges and the rights of non-black South Africans. The South African Broadcasting Corporation (SABC) is regarded as being the mouthpiece of the ANC.

Key words

Black Transformation: Government legislation to ensure that senior posts in the public and private sector reflect the racial composition of South Africa.

Social and economic issues

In 1994 the new ANC Government promised 'a job, a decent home and a chicken in every pot'. Clearly this has not been achieved and South Africa is in many ways more unequal than it was in 1994. However, the blame cannot be placed just on the white community. A new group of very wealthy blacks called the Black Diamonds now exists, yet the majority of blacks still experience unemployment and poverty.

Wealth and employment

The Government uses positive discrimination legislation, which favours non-whites in areas such as entry to higher education, employment opportunities and in the allocation of government contracts.

Many whites argue that reverse racism now exists because Black Economic Empowerment (BEE) legislation, including the Employment Equity Act, aims to create a more even society and to ensure that all employment, especially senior management posts, reflects the racial balance. These laws have enabled educated non-whites to acquire wealth through appointment to the top posts in universities, the civil service, police and health care.

However, there is doubt about the effectiveness of the legislation, with critics reporting that the majority of blacks have not benefited. Black unemployment is officially 30% but the actual figure is probably closer to 40%.

Black Diamonds

The Black Diamonds is a new group of around 4 million black people with top jobs in industry or government. They live in the most affluent areas of South Africa's cities; their children get the best state or private education; and they have access to the best medical treatment through private health insurance. In the past ten years the number of black millionaires has almost trebled. However, the discrimination against whites explains the decline in the white population, especially its millionaires.

Race	2007		2016	
	Number	%	Number	%
White people	36,600	86	21,200	56
Black people	6,200	14	17,300	44

Table 9.4 Millionaires in South Africa, 2007 and 2016

Wealth inequalities

The wealth gap between white people, the new black elite and the poor of all colours is widening in South Africa. However, thanks to government social grants, severe poverty has declined from 40% in 2001 to 10% today.

The unemployment figure is around 40%, but the official figure is given as 25%. The figures for unemployed young people are even higher.

Government support for the poor and unemployed is paid through social grants that help people with basic living expenses. During 1999, the number of people who benefited from grants was 2.5 million; in 2016 the figure was over 13 million. The majority of grants are child support, which was claimed by 7.8 million families in 2007 compared to 34,000 in 1999.

Policies and progress in education

- The Government doubled spending on education between 2008 and 2014. In 2016, public spending on education was 6.4% of gross domestic product (GDP); the average spending in EU countries is 4.8%.
- Additional funding has been given to poorer schools with savings made by the ending of segregated education.
- More schools now have electricity, water and sanitation. There are now fewer than 40% of schools without these facilities.
- 65% of higher education places are taken up by black South African students.
- In 1996, the grade 12 matriculation pass rate was 48.9%. In 2016 it had risen to 72%.
- Free education now reaches poor urban and rural areas, allowing more students to go to school. In 2002, the percentage of children in these areas completing compulsory schooling was 7%; by 2015 it had increased to over 65%.
- From 2018 free higher education will be provided for poor students whose family income is less than 150,000 rand per annum. In 2016 students had complained about high fees and this had resulted in protest marches and clashes between students and police.

Education problems

- There are major inequalities with regard to education provision between the provinces. For example, 96% of schools in the Western Cape have electricity, while just 40% do in the Eastern Cape.
- There are major inequalities with regard to exam results. The pass rate in Gauteng is 78% or above, while in Limpopo it is 58%.
- The all-black schools in rural areas or townships have the poorest results, while the former all-white or private schools with a mixture of students of all races show the best results.
- Skilled workers are in very short supply but millions of semi-literate unskilled people are unemployed.
- In a league table of educational performance in 2015, South Africa ranked 75th out of 76.

- In November 2016 the findings of an international comparison study in maths and science were shocking with regards to South African children. A staggering 27% of pupils who have attended school for six years cannot read compared to 4% in Tanzania.
- Only 35% of black children starting school go on to pass the matriculation exam and just 4% achieve a degree.

Why is South Africa's education failing compared to other African countries?

The culture of corruption and lack of accountability fostered by President Zuma and ANC officials is to blame. Much of the massive spending on education does not reach the classroom as outlined below:

- The Department of Education is run by party officials who do not have the experience or skills to run such a complex education system.
- Teachers pay union officials for head teacher posts and then proceed to raid the school budget.
- Funds from the central Government to pay for the education of the poorest students often do not reach the schools.
- Books and stationery often do not reach the schools.
- Many teachers are under-qualified and absenteeism among staff can be as high as 30% on a Friday or Monday.
- The teaching unions are too powerful and in 2016 forced the Government to cancel standardised testing.

Policies and progress in health

- Primary health care has been improved significantly, in part by the provision of clean water to 9 million black South Africans. This has had a major effect on child mortality rates, which double when there is no clean water access.
- More than 6 million children who go to primary school benefit from food and education due to the National Primary School Nutrition project, which provides a 'Mandela sandwich' to attendees.
- Pregnant women and children under six are entitled to free health care.
- Over 2 million citizens receive free anti-HIV/AIDS drugs.

HIV/AIDS in South Africa

South Africa faces an HIV/AIDS crisis. Six million black South Africans suffer from HIV/AIDS and life expectancy dropped from 62 years in 1993 to 51 years in 2005, largely under the leadership of President Mbeki.

The Government of Thabo Mbeki was criticised for failing to give free anti-AIDS drugs to all HIV-positive pregnant women and their children. President Zuma has ensured free treatment for HIV-positive babies and pregnant women and more than 2 million South Africans now receive anti-AIDS drugs. The success of these actions is reflected in the increase of life expectancy from 54 years in 2007 to 59 years in 2016, and also in a significant decrease in infant and under-five mortality.

AIDS pandemic

- Each year more than 60,000 children aged between a month and five years old die from AIDS or related illnesses.
- UNAIDS estimates that just under 6 million South Africans are living with HIV.
- The mothers of more than 1 million children under the age of eighteen have died from AIDS.

Private health provision creates health inequalities between the rich and the poor that inevitably reflect a racial imbalance in favour of white people and ensures that they have access to better health provision. However, the growing number of Black Diamonds means that more than 9 million people have private cover. Yet this still leaves 46 million people dependent on an over-stretched national health service.

Housing

- The Government has built more than 4 million homes with access to electricity since 1994. Soweto is an example of a once poor township that now has a shopping mall and modern housing with electricity.
- The number of black property owners increased by more than 80% between 2000 and 2014.
- More than 10 million homes now have clean water due to the Community Water Supply programme.
- According to a recent census, 85% of households in South Africa now have access to electricity and 90% of homes have access to water.

Population movement: informal settlements and segregation

The significant movement of people from the countryside to urban areas and the influx of immigrants has led to the creation of thousands of informal settlements ('squatter camps'). Their makeshift homes lack electricity and sanitation provision, crime is high and health is poor. Schooling is basic and many of the children do not complete secondary school and do not have the skills to contribute to or benefit from the BEE programmes. Gauteng and North West have the largest number of informal settlements, with one in five of their citizens trapped in these poverty zones.

Vast housing inequalities exist both between provinces and between races. While 98% of households in the Western Cape have access to piped water, only 62% of households in the Eastern Cape have such access.

Racial segregation still exists. While the new rich black South African elite have moved into the former white areas with their swimming pools and servants, the majority of black South Africans still live in segregated townships or informal settlements with limited facilities.

Land

Around 75,000 out of 80,000 claims for land re-distribution have been settled, yet black African ownership of land has increased from 13% to only 21% (the target set in 1994 was to redistribute 30% by 2004). Many black South Africans prefer financial compensation instead of being given land.

In 2005, the Constitutional Court confirmed the rights of white farmers against land invasion. The 'willing buyer–willing seller' principle will only be accepted if the farmer accepts a fair price. If this is rejected by the seller, the Constitution permits land to be taken by compulsory sale.

Crime and the law

Many South Africans live in absolute fear and this was the defence offered by the famous disabled athlete Oscar Pistorius, after he shot dead his girlfriend in 2013, believing her to be an intruder. South Africa has the tenth highest murder rate in the world (on average 44 murders take place every day) and violence against women, especially rape, is widespread.

In a 2013 opinion poll, two-thirds of South Africans thought the most corrupt officials are in the police. Top posts in the public sector, including the police, are given to ANC politicians who lack experience and qualifications. All three national police commissioners appointed since 2000 have ended up being fired for either incompetence or criminal behaviour. No police officers have been charged with the death of 34 striking miners who were attacked by the police in 2012.

Why is crime so high in South Africa?

- It is very easy to obtain guns and other weapons; this is as a result of the years of apartheid during which a violent culture was created in South Africa.
- Some people see inequalities with regard to wealth as a reason for violence, a 'war' between those who have and those who have not.
- Certain groups ignore the laws of the society, for example illegal immigrants and poor people who migrate from the countryside to the towns.
- Conviction rates, especially for rape, are very low. In a 2017 report, researchers found that of 500 sexual-assault cases reported to the police in Diepsloot since 2013 only one resulted in conviction.

Government action

- Police budgets have been significantly increased, leading to a rise in the number of officers available. Crime did significantly decline prior to and after the 2010 FIFA World Cup, which was held in South Africa.
- The Government claims that there has been a reduction in crime and official statistics support this claim, with the number of murders declining by 35% since 1994. However, the public does not share this perception that the streets are safer and argues that many crimes are not reported.

Influence over other countries

It could be argued that South Africa is a regional superpower. It produces two-thirds of the GDP of the countries of Southern Africa. South Africa also provides military support to assist the peace-keeping action of the **African Union**. It has played a key role in seeking to end various African conflicts in countries such as Burundi.

- South Africa is the only country in sub-Saharan Africa to be a member of the G20 group and the only African nation to have hosted the football World Cup, which took place in 2010.
- South Africa is an active member of the United Nations and was elected in 2006 and in 2010 to serve on the Security Council. However, it has been criticised for placing its loyalties with countries of the developing world ahead of human rights issues. In 2017, President Zuma welcomed to South Africa Omar al-Bashir, the president of Sudan, who has been accused by the International Criminal Court (ICC) of war crimes.
- South Africa is a member of the BRICS bloc (Brazil, Russia, India, China and South Africa). The BRICS bloc represents 43% of the world's population. South Africa sees its role as promoting the Africa agenda and representing the 1 billion African people.
- South Africa has used its military power to support UN peace-keeping forces in the Democratic Republic of the Congo (DRC). In 2013 a 3000-strong South African intervention force carried out offensive operations against rebel groups in Eastern DRC.

Key words

African Union (AU): A union consisting of 54 African states whose role is to provide 'African solutions to African problems', to support economic growth and to achieve conflict resolutions between states.

Questions and model answers

Describe question

There are many opportunities for people to participate in the political system.

Describe, **in detail**, at least **two** ways that people in a world power that you have studied can participate in the political system. **6 marks**

Remember

Knowledge and understanding questions will have 4, 6 or 8 marks allocated and you will need to answer three questions 'describing' or 'explaining'.

Model answer

South African people can participate in the political system by voting for or joining a political party. Most black South Africans support the ANC as it is the party of liberation. The most popular party for whites, coloureds and Asians is the Democratic Alliance. The DA is the most popular party in the Western Cape. The PR election system used encourages people to vote as most votes count. If a party gets 5% of the votes it will get 5% of the seats. ⇨

South Africans have the opportunity to participate in many elections every five years to elect representatives to the National Assembly and to the provincial assemblies as well as their councillors in local government elections. However, there are concerns that the ANC has too much power. It is in control of eight of the nine provinces and has complete control of the National Assembly and the president always belongs to the ANC. So this could lead to apathy.

Marker's comment

In this answer, two factors are described. The first paragraph would get 3 marks because it accurately identifies voting or joining a political party and highlights the main political parties. Further exemplification is provided with reference to voting choice being based on race.

The second paragraph would also get 3 marks because it accurately identifies the range of voting opportunities in South Africa. This is further developed in detail by referring to the dominance of the ANC with evidence that they control eight of the nine provinces.

Overall a very good and high-quality answer deserving of full marks.

6 marks

Hints & tips

- *Always structure your answers in paragraphs. Avoid list-type answers or bullet points.*
- *Make sure you take account of how many marks a question is worth. You should base the length of your answers on the time you should allocate to 4-mark, 6-mark or 8-mark questions.*

Explain question

Social and economic inequalities exist in all world powers.

Explain, **in detail**, why social and economic inequalities exist in a world power you have studied. **6 marks**

Remember

For a 6-mark answer you must cover at least two factors in depth. In an explain question, a maximum of 4 marks can be given for each detailed point you give, depending on their quality, level of detail, relevance, accuracy and exemplification. In your answer, it is also good to show the interaction of various factors.

Model answer

In South Africa the legacy of apartheid has created wealth inequalities between most black people and white people. Unemployment among black people is estimated to be as high as 40%, with millions of black people depending on government social grants for survival – over 13 million people receive these funds. The creation of a very wealthy black group called the Black Diamonds has widened inequalities in South Africa. There are about 4 million Black Diamonds in South Africa and many of them are millionaires.

Inequalities also exist in health. Most white people and Black Diamonds have private health care and go to the best hospitals in South Africa. The national health service is short-staffed and lacks resources. Many poor black people who live in poverty suffer from HIV/AIDS and cannot afford to buy the correct medicines and so their health suffers.

Marker's comment

In this answer the first paragraph would get 3 marks because in the first sentence it accurately links the legacy of apartheid to wealth inequalities/unemployment as a reason why social and economic inequalities remain. This is developed in detail with reference to social grants and the contrast with the Black Diamonds.

The second paragraph would also get 3 marks because it accurately identifies health inequalities as reasons why social and economic inequalities remain. This is developed and exemplified with reference to private health care for white people and Black Diamonds and the poor state of the South African national health service.

So, overall a very good and high-quality answer deserving of full marks.

6 marks

Chapter 10
World Powers: The People's Republic of China

What you should know

To be successful in this section, you should be able to **know** and **understand**:

★ the Chinese political system:
  - ★ the role and powers of the Chinese Communist Party and its total control of the Chinese Government at national, regional and local levels
  - ★ the participation and representation of the Chinese people in decision-making

★ the impact of the following social and economic issues:
  - ★ employment
  - ★ poverty/inequality
  - ★ population movement
  - ★ health
  - ★ education
  - ★ crime and law

★ the influence of China on other countries in the following spheres:
  - ★ political influence
  - ★ economic influence
  - ★ military influence.

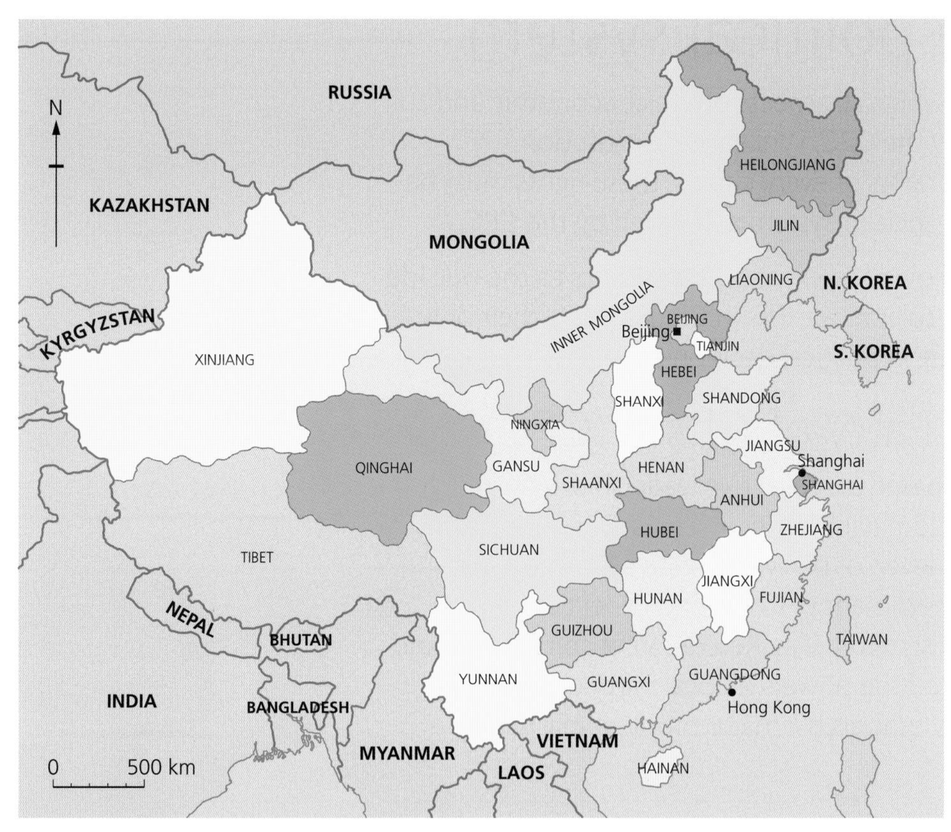

Figure 10.1 Map of China

Key features of China

- China is the third largest country in the world by area and its 1.3 billion citizens make it the most populous country in the world.
- China is made up of numerous nationalities. The Han Chinese make up 95% of the population. In 2013, China's urban population outnumbered the rural population for the first time.
- China is a communist country with its **ideology** based on the teachings of Marx, Lenin and Mao. (To widen your understanding of this ideology, you could undertake personal background research on these three prominent historical leaders.) The role of the Communist Party of China (CPC) is to guide and rule on behalf of the Chinese people and to protect socialist collective values such as placing the needs of society before selfish individual desires.
- Over the last fifteen years China's economy has more than quadrupled. In 2010 it overtook Japan to become the world's second largest economy.
- China has managed to introduce 'capitalist' changes to its economy without introducing political change. The CPC has loosened economic and social control in the country, while retaining total political control. Dissent is not tolerated and China has a poor human rights record.
- The present Chinese leader is Xi Jinping who replaced Hu Jintao in 2012. Both leaders have continued the economic reforms of Deng Xiaoping who ruled China from 1978 until his death in 1997. Mao's slogan was 'Serve the people'; Deng's was 'To get rich is glorious'.

Key words

Ideology: A set of political beliefs which guides the government of a country.

The Chinese political system

China is a one-party state in which all aspects of social, economic and political life are dominated by the CPC. While the Constitution guarantees 'the fundamental rights of every citizen', these rights must be used to support the Chinese socialist system as defined by the CPC.

Smaller political parties are allowed to exist as this presents to the outside world an image that political tolerance exists in China. This is their only function and they play no part in political decision-making.

The Communist Party of China (CPC)

The leadership of the CPC is based on collective leadership. However, it is clear that President Xi is the dominant leader in China. The decisions of the leaders are binding on all levels of party and state structures. The party leaders are also the Government of China and expect strict obedience from all party and state officials. Relaxation of some social and economic controls has reduced the powers of local party officials. However, corruption by party officials is a major problem in China.

The new emperor of China – Xi Jinping

President Xi has acquired more powers than any other Chinese leader since the death of Mao in 1976. Since January 2016 President Xi Jinping has replaced 20 of the Communist Party's 31 provincial secretaries and has used his campaign against party corruption not just to punish the guilty but to dismiss many who criticise his actions, including leaders of the armed forces and Mr Zhou, who was in charge of national security. He has been accused of abandoning the Party's system of 'collective responsibility' by extending his powers and to condoning a personality cult. The official media refer to him as 'Uncle Xi'.

He is not only party leader, head of state and commander-in-chief but has set up new committees which give him total control over state security and the economy. The prime minister, Li Keqiang, has been sidelined. President Xi has also enforced strict political control over the Chinese people and, for example, arrested lawyers trying to protect the rights of the Chinese people.

Figure 10.2 President Xi Jinping

Executive branch	Legislative branch	Judicial branch
Head of state: President Xi Jinping	Unicameral	Supreme People's Court
Head of government: Premier Li Keqiang	National People's Congress (3000 members)	Judges appointed by the National People's Congress

Table 10.1 The three branches of central government

Xi Jinping
- General Secretary of Communist Party of China (CPC)
- Head of military
- President of China

↓

Standing Committee (Politburo)
- 7 members – reduced by Xi from 9

↓

Politburo
- 25 members – equivalent to the UK cabinet

↓

CPC Central Committee
- Approximately 360 members

↓

National Congress of CPC
- Only meets every 5 years and rubber stamps the next 5-year plan of the party leaders

↓

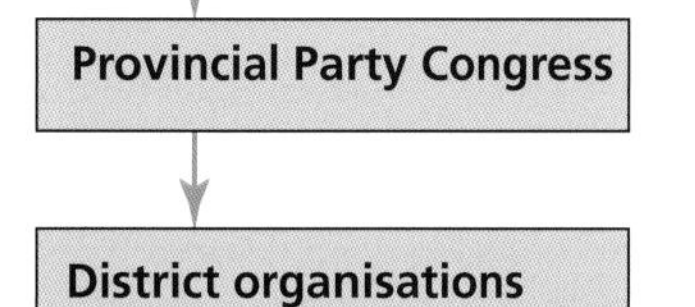

Provincial Party Congress

↓

District organisations

↓

City and town party organisations

↓

Party sections in the workplace

Figure 10.3 Organisation of the Communist Party of China

Elections

- The president and vice president are 'elected' by the National People's Congress (NPC) for five-year terms.
- The premier is nominated by the president and confirmed by the NPC for five-year terms.
- Members of the NPC are elected by regional and provincial people's congresses to serve five-year terms.

Participation and representation in China

The Chinese Constitution provides a wide range of political and social rights. According to Article 35, Chinese citizens have the right to:

- 'freedom of speech, of the press, of assembly, of association and of demonstration'.

However, all political and social rights must support the values of China's socialist system and individuals must be responsible citizens (see Table 10.2).

Rights	Responsibilities
To hold protests and demonstrations that support the socialist system, for example take part in marches organised by the Party against actions by foreign countries such as Japan or Vietnam.	You must obtain permission of party officials first and act peacefully. Even standing outside the courts to provide support to an individual accused of crimes against the state is illegal.
To submit petitions to the Chinese Government, either written or an e-petition, to address an injustice.	You must provide your name, address and passport number for identification so that you can be traced.
To vote in elections at the local level and to stand as a candidate.	To turn out to vote and to ensure that if you wish to stand your views reflect party directives.
To join the CPC and to promote socialist values.	It is very difficult to join the CPC with only 5% of the population being members.
To practise a religion (under Article 36 of the Constitution).	You can only practise your religion if it is one of the permitted religions controlled by the Party, otherwise you will be persecuted.
To join a trade union in your place of work.	You can only join a trade union controlled by the Party.
To access old and new media (China has the world's largest population of internet users: 690 million in 2016. Complaints that were once local are now debated nationwide.)	Newspapers are controlled by the state and are propaganda tools of the state. The internet is also censored with an army of officials scrutinising all websites.
Provinces with a majority of ethnic minorities such as Tibet and Xinjiang should be granted devolved powers.	The CPC only appoint Han Chinese to administer these provinces. In reality the Chinese military control the activities of the local people.

Table 10. 2 The responsibilities and limitations to rights of Chinese citizens

Hong Kong – 'one country, two systems'

Only in Hong Kong do Chinese citizens experience some of the political freedoms that exist in Western democracies. The 6 million citizens in Hong Kong can vote for different political parties, criticise the Chinese Government, read a free press, expect an impartial judge and take part in protest marches such as those held to remember the Tiananmen Square massacre of 1989.

Hong Kong was a colony of Britain until it returned to Chinese rule in 1997. Under the 1997 agreement, Hong Kong was given a 'high degree of autonomy'. However, the administration of Hong Kong must be approved by the Chinese leaders and its citizens cannot elect their leaders.

In July 2017 China's 'Nelson Mandela', Liu Xiaobo, died in a 'prison' hospital. Liu's crime was to write a petition calling for democracy; the Government response was an eleven-year sentence for subversion. Despite having terminal liver cancer, Liu was refused permission to go with his family to America for treatment. The death of this Nobel Peace Prize winner was mourned in the West but completely ignored in China. An army of internet censors deleted any reference to his death and ensured that his widow remained in isolation under house arrest. Such is the economic dominance of China that world leaders refrained from criticising China's actions.

Figure 10.4 Liu Xiaobo

Dissent in China

The US Congress tries to maintain a database on the number of political prisoners in China. Below are some of its findings over the decades:

- More than 10,000 Falun Gong members were detained between 1999 and 2010; of these, one-fifth may have died in prison.
- Prior to the Olympic games being held in China in 2008, thousands of dissidents were arrested or placed under house arrest. In Tibet alone in 2008, just under a thousand Tibetans were arrested for protesting against Chinese control.
- Under President Xi, new security laws have been introduced; for example, it is now illegal to gather outside a court during a political trial. Lawyers who defend those charged are now being accused of 'subverting state power'.
- Individuals who spread information about social problems such as pollution are now being arrested.

Social and economic issues

China's massive economic growth over the last 30 years has brought wealth to millions and has transformed the landscape of China. While it has created a strong wealthy middle class, China is now one of the most unequal societies in the world.

Employment and income

In 1990 a Chinese middle class barely existed; today it stands at 260 million. The policies begun by Deng to open trade with the world and to allow private enterprise to flourish have created the Chinese economic miracle and a consumer explosion. It is estimated that China now has over 250 billionaires. The average annual income of a Chinese citizen is around $7200; in 1990 it was around $1200.

Poverty and inequality

Vast inequalities exist between urban and rural areas and between coastal and inland provinces. There is also massive inequality between urban migrant workers and permanent city residence (see 'The *hukou* system').

- Permanent residents in coastal provinces are far richer than citizens of the remote province of Xin Jiang, for example. Shanghai, which is counted as a province, is five times wealthier than the poorest province, Gansu, which has a similar-sized population.
- The average income of people in the countryside is only a third of the average urban income.

The *hukou* system

This system manages the movement of an estimated 280 million rural citizens to the cities in search of work. All Chinese citizens receive a residence permit based on their place of birth – the *hukou*. This penalises the migrant workers who, encouraged by the Government, move into the cities to provide the cheap labour that has created China's economic miracle. Because they are defined as having a rural *hukou*, the migrant workers are denied full access to hospitals and welfare services. If the migrants bring their families with them, then their children also suffer as they are denied a free education and health provision. Migrant workers often live in grim conditions, in tiny brick shacks with little sanitation. If the workers have left their families behind, they live in austere overcrowded barracks provided by their employer. These living arrangements are hidden from the view of tourists.

Effectiveness in tackling poverty/inequality

- The 'Go West' strategy involves the building of roads, pipelines and other investments in inland provinces to provide employment and to stimulate their economies.
- Twinning arrangements with provinces and cities in rich coastal areas provide financial aid and advice to inland provinces.
- Central government provides extra money to poorer provinces. Ten of China's 33 provinces receive more than half of their budgets from this source.
- Provincial inequalities halved between 2000 and 2015, and a significant rebalance has been achieved. However, China's recent decline in economic growth has halted the trend in redistribution of wealth.
- At present property ownership only exists in urban areas. In the countryside the land is collectively owned. Allowing farmers to own and sell land would improve housing stock and enable migrant workers to sell their property and increase their incomes.
- Between 1980 and 2010, China reduced the number of people living below the poverty line by 600 million. (The official poverty line is an annual income of 2300 yuan.) This was achieved by a massive programme of public works which boosted employment and income. In October 2015, President Xi stated that China would eradicate poverty by 2020.
- For those still experiencing poverty, the state provides a 'subsistence guarantee' referred to as *dibao*, which is administered by local government. By 2015, the *dibao* provided financial support for 55 million mostly rural inhabitants. Two-thirds of those who were below the poverty line on joining the scheme are now above it.

Reform of the *hukou* system

Aware of the growing unrest among migrant workers, the Government is now committed to providing equal rights for all urban workers. However, there is strong resistance from local government and arguments over who will pay the bill. Local residents are concerned that if migrants are given full rights, their own privileged access to education and health will be threatened.

- The new urbanisation policy calls for 100 million migrants to be given urban *hukou* by 2020 but with the condition that applicants have a stable job and a legal place to live.
- Migrant workers' incomes have increased from an average monthly income of 140 yuan in 2009 to 250 yuan in 2017.

Health issues

- One-fifth of China's farmland contains higher than permitted levels of pollutants, some of which threaten food safety. Leaks from factories often seep into rice fields and contaminate the food chain. A recent report from a food standards investigation in Guangzhou, a southern city, discovered that nearly half of the rice tested by inspectors in restaurants and canteens was laced with cadmium.
- 40% of hospital budgets to pay staff come from selling medicine; less than 10% comes from the Government.

Government actions

- New community health centres have been built and subsidised insurance schemes have been expanded. By the end of 2014 over 95% of citizens had some form of insurance – up from 15% in 2000.
- China has created eco-city projects to provide a healthier environment for its citizens. It has imposed stricter controls on emissions of carbon and smog-forming pollutants.

Education issues

Urban/rural disparities

- Urban education is better financed than that in rural areas. In 2014 annual expenditure per child in a typical urban school was 20,000 yuan compared with just 3000 in a rural school.
- Completion of junior middle school (Primary 1 to S3 in Scotland) has been compulsory since 1986 and rural children now have a basic education. However, dropout rates are high with about one in six rural pupils not finishing junior school.
- The dropout rate is even higher in senior middle schools as most rural students have to leave home and board in the school. Tuition fees and the cost of books mean that poor families cannot afford to send their children to high school, assuming they have passed the entrance exam.

Migrant children

- Many migrant workers have no choice but to leave their children behind to be educated in the second-class rural schools. Children who move to the cities with their parents are denied entry to the state schools as they do not have an urban *hukou*.

Privileges of Party membership

- Entry to the top schools is automatic for the children and relatives of Party members. Those with wealth can also pay a bribe to admission officers of schools and universities to gain access for their children.

Effectiveness in tackling education issues

- Tuition and book fees have now been scrapped for primary and junior pupils, but senior students still have to pay, and the costs are higher.
- Universities are required to increase their quota of rural students.
- In 1990 just 7% of rural students completed senior middle school; by 2017 the figure had risen to one-third. In the large cities, over 90% of children with permanent residence complete senior middle school.

Population movement

In 1985, only 20% of the population lived in urban areas; in 2017 the figure stood at 54% and it is estimated to rise to 70% by 2020. This highlights the massive movement from the countryside to the towns. Many of these migrants have settled with their families in the cities but are second-class citizens because of the *hukou* system.

Han Chinese expansion

The central Government has moved millions of Han Chinese to the provinces with a very high ethnic minority population. In 1960 only 10% of the population of Xinnjiang was Han; in 2017 it was over 40%.

Growing gender and age imbalance

The introduction in the 1980s of the One Child Policy, which stated that couples in China were only allowed to have one child, has led to a significant increase in the number of boys compared to girls and to an ageing population. In 2014 there were 116 boys born for every 100 girls.

In October 2015 the Party announced that all families could now have two children. The policy had previously been relaxed to allow a parent who was an only child to have a second child.

However, a generation has been brought up indoctrinated in the belief that China 'had too many people'. As such, when the policy was relaxed in 2013 only 10% of those eligible applied.

Those who have more than two children will still be punished and so the 1-million-strong army of family planning officials continue to impose fines or forced abortions.

Crime and the law

Using our definition of criminal offences, China has a very low crime rate and is a very safe place to live – given the level of government surveillance, a wise citizen obeys the laws of the country. With 50 crimes carrying the death penalty and with the imposition of harsh sentences, deterrence seems to be effective.

Cybercrime

This is a growing problem in all countries, with criminal gangs stealing individual and company assets.

Human trafficking

With the shortage of women in the population, criminals are engaged in kidnapping women and selling them as brides in remote areas where they will never be found.

Influence on other countries

China's influence over the international community has been growing both politically and economically. The political and economic disintegration of the Soviet Union in the 1990s justified the view that the USA was the only superpower. China is the new emerging superpower and has replaced Russia in terms of world influence. It has the largest army in the world and is also a nuclear power.

- China is a permanent member of the Security Council of the United Nations. It is also the biggest contributor to UN peacekeeping missions and takes part in anti-piracy patrols off the Horn of Africa. China has used the veto to protect itself or obstruct the global interests of the USA. It sometimes works in partnership with Russia and recognised Russia's occupation of Crimea (taken from Ukraine).
- China is a key member of the G20 group of dominant nations. It is committed to reducing global pollution by signing up to the Paris Climate Agreement. It is also a key player in ensuring global economic stability.
- China's economy is second to that of the USA. China has investments in numerous countries and its products are sold around the world. It has increased its influence among African nations by paying to extract their raw materials.
- China is challenging the American-led world order in Asia. In 2014 China helped to set up SCO (Shanghai Cooperation Organisation). This consists of six countries – China, Russia, Kazakhstan, Kyrgyzstan, Tajikistan and Uzbekistan – and aims to be the dominant security institution in that region.
- China has challenged US military dominance in the western Pacific by pursuing an aggressive expansionist policy. In the South China Sea, where various atolls are claimed by several Asian states, China has engaged in an island-building frenzy in disputed waters, turning some into land masses large enough to welcome Chinese fighter jets. China is also in dispute with Vietnam over territorial waters.
- China has the largest army in the world and is modernising its navy to challenge America's maritime dominance. It now has its own aircraft carrier, with more to follow; the USA has ten, including four in the Pacific.

Country	Size of armed forces (millions)
China	3.0
India	2.7
USA	1.4
North Korea	1.3

Table 10.3 World's largest armed forces (millions)

Questions and model answers

Describe question

Governments have tried to tackle social and economic inequality.

Describe, **in detail**, **two** ways in which the government of the world power you have studied has tried to tackle social and economic inequality. **6 marks**

Model answer

In China, there are massive social and economic inequalities between those who live in coastal provinces and those who live in the inland provinces. One policy has been to engage in a massive investment programme in the inland western provinces. This has provided employment to local workers and increased their wealth. Roads, schools and hospitals have been built. This has improved the people's health and the quality of education.

The Government also provides extra money to the poorer provinces and this also has helped to reduce social and economic inequalities. The 10 poorest of the 33 provinces receive half of all government funding. This extra money is used to provide employment and to improve schools and health provision.

Marker's comment

This answer examines provincial inequalities and covers two policies in detail. The first paragraph would get 3 marks because it accurately identifies government action to address inequalities with excellent exemplification.

Further exemplification is provided in paragraph two with reference to funding allocation to the poorer provinces.

Overall a very good and high-quality answer deserving of full marks. **6 marks**

Remember

In a describe question, up to 3 marks can be awarded for each description you make, depending on their quality, level of detail, relevance, accuracy and exemplification.

Explain question

Some groups of people are more likely to participate in politics than others.

Explain, **in detail**, why some groups of people in the world power you have studied are more likely to participate than others. **6 marks**

Model answer

Members of the Communist Party are more likely to engage in politics as they can influence decision-making and become very powerful citizens. They can attend local and provincial party conferences and if they are favoured by their leaders could influence policy at the national level by being chosen to attend the National Party Congress or even being appointed to the Central Committee or Politburo.

In contrast, ethnic minorities such as Tibetans are far less likely to participate as they feel they are second-class citizens in their own provinces. The leaders of their provinces are all appointed by the Communist Party and all are Han Chinese. If they protest and demand their political rights, they will be arrested and put into prison. They have no influence.

Marker's comment

In this answer the candidate provides excellent contrast between two groups of people – Party members and ethnic minorities. The first paragraph would get 3 marks because it displays excellent knowledge and understanding of the structure of the CPC. It also highlights the political influence of party members.

The second paragraph would also get 3 marks because it accurately identifies the political barriers facing ethnic minorities. It uses Tibet to exemplify that the local people have no political influence and that they will be punished if they challenge the CPC.

Overall a very good and high-quality answer deserving of full marks. **6 marks**

Hints & tips

Always structure your answers in paragraphs. Avoid list-type answers or bullet points.

Hints & tips

Make sure you take account of how many marks a question is worth. You should base the length of your answers on the time you should allocate to 4-mark, 6-mark or 8-mark questions.

Remember

For a 3-mark answer you must cover at least two factors in depth. In an explain question, a maximum of 4 marks can be given for each detailed point you give, depending on their quality, level of detail, relevance, accuracy and exemplification. In your answer, it is also good to show the interaction of various factors.

Remember

Knowledge and understanding questions will have 4, 6 or 8 marks allocated and you will need to answer three questions.

Chapter 11
World Issues: Development Issues in Africa

What you should know

To be successful in this section, you should **know** and **understand**:

★ the economic, social and political factors affecting development
★ the consequences of the lack of development on the African people
★ the ways in which human rights in Africa are compromised
★ how developed nations are working to help Africa
★ how international organisations, such as the following, are working to help Africa:
  ★ African Union
  ★ UN specialised agencies and NGOs
★ the successes and failures of an international organisation's response to development issues.

Remember

Relevant examples from the countries of Africa are important when answering exam questions. You will find useful examples throughout this revision text.

Developed and developing countries

	Developed countries	Developing countries
Key terms	• Rich North • First World	• Poor South • Third World
Characteristics	• High standard of living • Good health services • High literacy levels • Low infant mortality rates • Economies based on industry, trade and new technologies • Democratic	• Low standard of living • Poor health care services • Low literacy levels (high illiteracy) • High infant mortality rates • Economies based on agriculture, and there is a lack of modern technology and labour skills • Corrupt governments
Countries	UK, USA, France, Germany, Australia, Japan and Canada	Nigeria, Sudan, Angola, DRC, Chad and Mali

Table 11.1 Developed and developing nations

Background

In total, around 1 billion people live in the continent of Africa, which is made up of 54 independent countries.

Although Africa is rich in natural resources, such as oil, diamonds, gold, iron, timber and tropical fruits, eighteen of the twenty poorest countries in the world are in sub-Saharan Africa and around 70% of Africa's population lives on less than $2 a day. More than 40% of the population is under fifteen years of age in many African countries, particularly those below the Sahara desert.

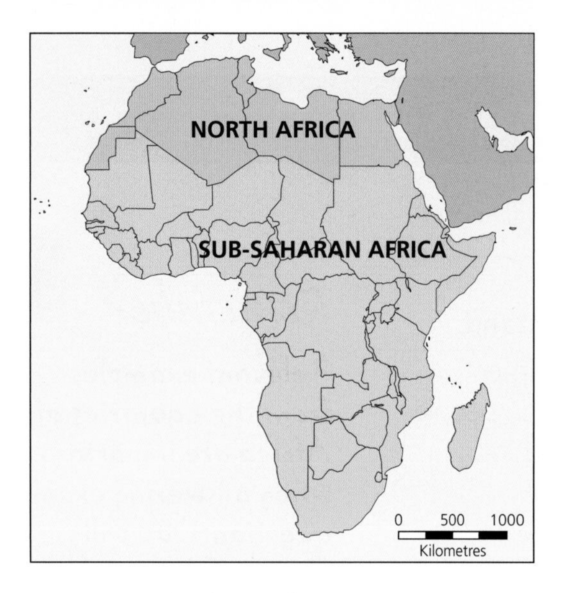

Figure 11.1 Sub-Saharan Africa

Causes of underdevelopment in Africa

Economic factors

Debt

Developing world debt is a major obstacle to human development. In total, Africa has a debt of $300 billion, and the 54 countries spend on average $14 billion annually just to repay this debt. This means they have less to spend on schools and hospitals.

Many African governments have borrowed money to finance development from the International Monetary Fund (IMF) or the World Bank, and this has to be repaid. Africa has also had its problems with odious debt, which is debt that has been loaned to corrupt African governments by rich nations that has then been misspent.

Trade

Given its natural resources, Africa should be a wealthy continent with many products available to trade and sell to the rest of the world. If Africa earned more through trade, its countries would be able to use the profits rather than rely on foreign aid and loans.

In Africa, trade varies greatly from country to country. For example, Sudan and Nigeria have large oil reserves and can export millions of barrels of oil per day, whereas Malawi and Ethiopia depend on growing and exporting cash crops like tea and coffee. However, the prices of cash crops can be forced down by buyers and this reduces the amount of money going into the developing countries. Many African nations also lack the infrastructure to transport goods and this makes trade between African countries difficult.

Political factors

Armed conflict

A country's social and economic development will be affected by armed conflict. For many decades some African nations, including the Democratic Republic of the Congo (DRC), Sudan, Somalia and Rwanda, have been engaged in **civil war**. These wars can continue for a long time and it can take a country years to recover and rebuild after the conflict has ended.

Key words

Civil war: A war between groups, factions or inhabitants within the same country.

Corruption and bad governance

A country will suffer if taxes are not collected to spend on public services, for example hospitals and schools. This is an example of bad governance. Another example would be if the military, the police or the legal system do not operate in a fair and impartial way, so treating people unjustly and depriving them of some human rights.

The lack of democracy in many African states has meant that corrupt dictators have been able to remain in power, using money meant for the country to fund their own lavish lifestyles while the citizens suffer. It is estimated that corruption in Africa costs around $150 billion a year. In 2017, Somalia was deemed to be the most corrupt country in the world according to the annual Corruption Perception Index.

Social factors

Health

In Africa around 1 million people died of AIDS in 2017 and an estimated 1.5 million were newly infected. Approximately 25 million people are currently living with HIV/AIDS in sub-Saharan Africa. Swaziland, a small landlocked country in southern Africa, has the highest HIV prevalence in the world, with 28.8% of their adult population living with HIV.

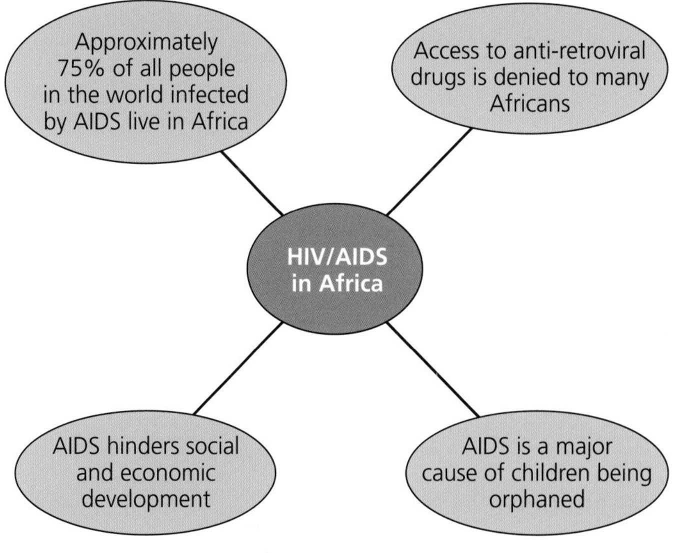

Figure 11.2 HIV/AIDS in Africa

Malaria is a disease transmitted by mosquitoes. It is one of the leading causes of death and disease in the developing world but it is preventable and treatable. Untreated malaria kills more than 1 million people each year, many of them in sub-Saharan Africa. Children under five are most at risk with 75% of deaths occurring in that age group.

Education

School enrolment in African countries is the lowest in the world, with 33 million children not attending primary school. Pupils who do attend school often do not have basic facilities or resources and can be in classes of between 40 and 70 pupils.

Other factors

Climate change

In parts of Kenya it has become 3.5°C hotter over the past twenty years. Changes in the weather make working the land and growing crops more difficult for farmers. This is causing unemployment, loss of earnings and **famine**.

Key words

Famine: An extreme shortage of food.

Natural disasters

Climate change is also a factor in droughts and flooding in Africa, which are becoming increasingly common. These have a major effect on people's lives as they affect food and water supplies as well as general everyday living. The financial cost of recovering from a natural disaster can exceed $1 billion and places enormous pressure on government resources.

What are the consequences of underdevelopment?

Create a spider diagram outlining the various causes of underdevelopment in Africa.

Lack of development has caused serious problems for the people of Africa, such as malnutrition, war and disease. This is an international issue that needs to be tackled immediately.

Lack of social services

Debt and trade issues mean that many African countries lack the type of social services we expect in Scotland. Schools often lack basic amenities such as electricity and running water. Hospitals are underfunded and under-resourced with too few doctors and nurses; many people living in rural areas have no educational or health facilities at all. Angola's debt highlights the problem – Angola spends 6.8% of its GDP on loan repayments and only 1.5% on health.

The impact of armed conflict

The impact of armed conflict within a country has devastating effects on the population. Civilians caught up in fighting can be killed or injured or have to flee their own homes to neighbouring countries. Unfortunately, at any one time there are numerous conflicts happening across the continent of Africa.

In Somalia, the lack of proper governance has meant a breakdown of law and order in many parts of the country. In the south there has been an ongoing war between government and African Union forces and Islamic militant groups. Islamic group al-Shabaab have control over large areas of territory and aim to fight until they can impose their strict vision of Islam on Somalia. In 2017, al-Shabaab killed over twenty African Union peacekeepers in a brutal ambush.

Child soldiers

Children are being forced to participate in wars, fighting as child soldiers, in some African countries. Around 60% of the 250,000 child soldiers in the world are thought to be in Africa. Child soldiers are currently being used in armed conflicts in the Central African Republic, Chad, DRC, Mali, Somalia and Sudan.

Many child soldiers suffer psychological effects for a long time after the fighting has ended. They are often badly affected by things they have done and seen and become desensitised to violence. Most child soldiers will have missed out on school and without an education they have very few future prospects.

Figure 11.3 Child soldiers in Africa

Disease and HIV/AIDS

Diseases such as malaria and the AIDS epidemic have had an enormous effect on social and economic development in Africa. They place a huge strain on medical services and hospitals are struggling to cope with the number of AIDS patients. Around one-third of the population of Botswana has the HIV virus, which prevents sufferers from working and contributing to the economy, and severely lowers life expectancy.

Famine and malnutrition

Famine can be the result of natural disaster, such as drought which causes low food production, or armed conflict where access to food is severely restricted. Around 275 million Africans are thought to go hungry every day and it is estimated that one-third of people living in sub-Saharan Africa are undernourished. Children are often victims of **malnutrition**. Poor nutrition is a major contributor to around 50% of child deaths in Africa. Malnutrition makes diseases such as measles and malaria much worse.

Key words

Malnutrition: A general term that indicates a lack of some or all nutritional elements necessary for human health.

Lack of human rights

Everyone is entitled to human rights. After the end of the Second World War, the United Nations made a list of basic rights that all humans should have. These were set out in the 1948 Universal Declaration of Human Rights. Some of these rights are as follows:

UN Universal Declaration of Human Rights

The right to life, liberty and security.

The right to take part in politics.

The right to freedom of speech.

The right to an education.

A lot of Africans will not be able to enjoy some of these human rights because of what is happening in their country. In every African country there is likely to be at least one factor to prevent citizens from accessing their full human rights as set out by the UN.

Right	How it is compromised
The right to life, liberty and security	This right will be compromised in an African country that is locked in conflict. The threat of violence and rape can be a daily worry for those in countries such as Sudan and Mali.
The right to take part in politics	Not every country in Africa has a democratic political system. In countries where there is a long established **dictatorship**, taking part in a fair political process will rarely happen.

Table 11.2 How human rights are compromised in Africa

Key words

Dictatorship: A form of government in which a person or a small group rules with almost unlimited power.

Create a spider diagram outlining the various consequences of underdevelopment in Africa.

Children's rights

The United Nations Convention on the Rights of the Child (CRC) gives all children the same rights based on what a child needs to survive, grow, participate and fulfil their potential. These rights apply equally to every child, regardless of where they are from or who they are. However, the chance of a child enjoying any or all of these rights is severely reduced if they are from Africa.

How has the international community responded to development issues in Africa?

Individual countries, non-governmental organisations (NGOs) and international organisations are all working to improve the situation in Africa and to address the many issues the continent faces.

Developed nations

Developed nations give aid, which can help poorer countries to overcome the challenges they face. Aid can be given in different forms, from humanitarian emergency assistance for disasters such as droughts or earthquakes, to longer-term development aid. It is important that the aid goes towards targeting the specific problems of that nation. There are three main types of aid as outlined in Table 11.3.

Type of aid	Source of aid	Description
Bilateral	From one government to another.	Developed countries will target specific countries that require aid. Britain's bilateral aid is organised by the Department for International Development (DFID).
Multilateral	Aid given by international organisations.	Multilateral aid is given by international organisations such as the European Union (EU) and the United Nations (UN).
Voluntary aid	Aid given by NGOs or charities.	Many NGOs, such as Oxfam, fund specialised projects in developing countries, such as building schools or installing water pumps.

Table 11.3 The different types of aid

Tied aid

Tied aid is bilateral aid that has conditions attached whereby the country receiving the aid must use it to buy services and goods from the donor country. The donor county also benefits in this type of situation.

Motivations for providing aid

Countries who give tied aid are motivated by what they receive in return for the aid they give. China, for example, provides aid to many African countries and although much of their aid isn't tied, China expects to gain politically and economically. Looking closer at what drives Chinese aid allocation to Africa, evidence shows that China provides more foreign aid to oil-rich African countries than those that are not oil rich. Almost half of the top ten recipients of Chinese aid in the past ten years gave China access to oil wells and granted first rights to future oil. Examples include Angola, Nigeria and Sudan.

However, most developed democratic countries like the UK are motivated to give aid to help and support developing nations, especially in times of emergency or crisis like a famine or a drought. They will not tie aid with conditions. Developed nations pledge to give a proportion of their wealth (usually 0.7% of Gross National Income, as agreed by the UN) as governments and citizens in the developed world want to help those less fortunate around the globe.

UK aid to African countries

The UK Department for International Development (DFID) promotes development in the developing world, particularly in countries where there is extreme poverty.

DFID works alongside charities, businesses and international organisations such as the World Bank and the UN to achieve the Sustainable Development Goals (SDGs) (see page 115).

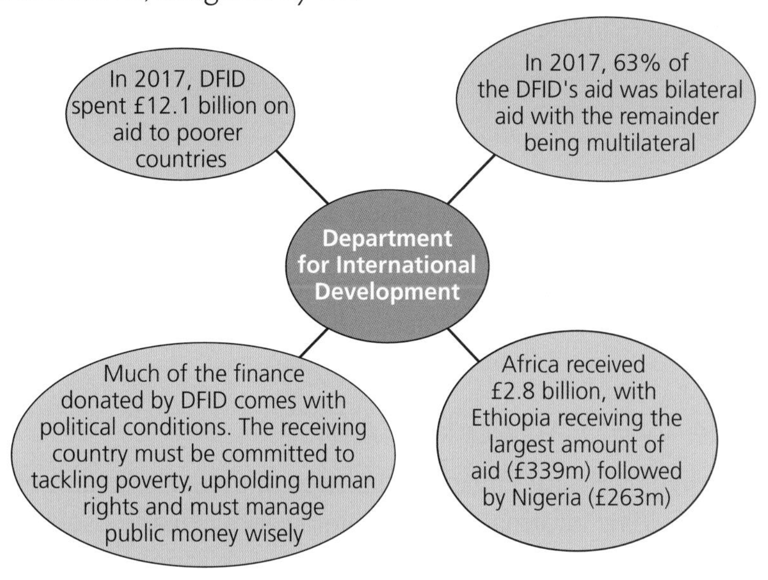

Figure 11.4 Some of the work of DFID

International organisations

The African Union (AU)

The AU promotes democracy and human rights in Africa by stimulating the economy. It was founded in 2002 to help bring peace to Africa by reducing conflict there. During times of conflict the AU will provide a military presence to protect the citizens of the countries involved. The AU worked with the Somali Government in 2018 to fight the terrorist group al-Shabaab, which tried to take over the country.

The United Nations (UN)

The United Nations deals with development issues in Africa. It was founded in 1945 and one of its main aims was to improve the lives of humans throughout the world by encouraging countries to work together. This is necessary in many African countries.

The UN has a number of specialised agencies that deliver multilateral aid and assistance when needed. Each agency has a specific focus when it comes to meeting the needs of developing nations.

- The United Nations Children's Fund (UNICEF)
- The Food and Agriculture Organization (FAO)
- The World Food Program (WFP)
- The International Labour Organization (ILO)
- The United Nations Educational, Scientific and Cultural Organization (UNESCO)
- The World Health Organization (WHO)

UNICEF in Africa

UNICEF works to improve the lives of children around the world. As a child dies every fifteen seconds in Africa, the job UNICEF does is vital in saving lives in the developing world.

UNICEF at work: Schools for Africa

Since Schools for Africa was launched, more than 12 million children have benefited from increased access to, and quality of, education. UNICEF has built 415 new classrooms in the remotest parts of Mali and Burkina Faso, as well as trained 10,000 teachers in Ethiopia, Mali, Malawi, Burkina Faso and Niger.

The WHO at work in Africa

The World Health Organization helps to meet the health needs of people by providing information and training about health issues. The WHO also carries out health care itself, such as immunisation campaigns to wipe out killer diseases like tuberculosis.

The WHO at work: tackling infant mortality

Between 2012 and 2017, the WHO engaged in an initiative aimed at assisting the most affected countries in sub-Saharan Africa to improve access to diagnosis and treatment for the major causes of death in children under five years of age: malaria, pneumonia and diarrhoea.

Sustainable Development Goals (SDGs)

In 2000, nearly 190 countries signed up to a range of goals and targets called the Millennium Development Goals, which were designed to reduce world poverty and hunger and improve the lives of people in the developing world. In 2015, these goals were revised and a new list drawn up called the **Sustainable Development Goals (SDGs)**. The new targets include fully eradicating extreme poverty while health targets include ending preventable deaths of newborns and children under five years old.

The seventeen SDGs include the following:

- End poverty in all its forms everywhere.
- End hunger, and achieve food security and improved nutrition.
- Ensure healthy lives and promote wellbeing for all at all ages.
- Ensure inclusive and equitable quality education and promote life-long learning opportunities.
- Achieve gender equality and empower all women and girls.
- Ensure availability and sustainable management of water and sanitation for all.
- Build infrastructure, promote inclusive and sustainable industrialisation and foster innovation.
- Reduce inequality within and among countries.
- Make cities and human settlements inclusive, safe, resilient and sustainable.
- Take urgent action to combat climate change and its impacts.

Non-governmental organisations (NGOs) in Africa

Many NGOs work in the developing world. You will learn about the role NGOs play in African development by focusing on the work of two major organisations: War Child and Oxfam.

- War Child deals with children in areas of conflict.
- Oxfam aims to fight poverty all over the world.

War Child at work: Uganda

In war-torn Uganda, War Child is providing 1500 children with pens, books and uniforms to enable them to get an education. In addition, War Child is training police, local courts and medical staff in Karamoja to improve their work for girls who have been raped. War Child is also providing equipment so clinics can treat and prevent STIs and unwanted pregnancies.

Oxfam

Oxfam tackles the main causes of poverty, from providing life's basics – food, water, health and education – to aid, climate change and human rights.

Oxfam at work: South Sudan

South Sudan is not only the world's newest nation but it is also one of the poorest. After almost 40 years of civil war, water, sanitation and health services in South Sudan are completely inadequate. Water-related diseases are rife, and one in seven children dies before the age of five. Oxfam is providing safe, clean water by building new watering holes in ten local communities. This means that families no longer have to walk miles to fetch water, freeing up their time for education, farming and developing livelihoods.

Activity

Create cue cards outlining the ways various international organisations have responded to the needs of Africa.

The successes and failures of NGOs in responding to development issues in Africa

The issues affecting Africa's development are immense and dwarf the resources of all NGOs, let alone one particular NGO like Oxfam. What is true, however, is that at their best NGOs can make a striking and important contribution to improving the lives and futures of many African people. The examples in the preceding case studies show how lives have been changed for the better. For example, without War Child more children would suffer the scars of conflict.

However, NGOs have their shortcomings. One growing concern is the so-called 'compassion fatigue' felt by the public as they are asked to donate to yet another important cause. Some NGOs are accused of spending too much on administration, which can put people off donating. Other NGOs are well meaning, but lack expertise and fall short of the standards expected of an aid organisation. In comparison to the UN and international governments, individual NGOs operate on a small scale and consequently their impact is inevitably limited.

Questions and model answers

Remember

Knowledge and understanding questions will have 4, 6 or 8 marks allocated and you will need to answer two or three questions 'describing' or 'explaining'. You must give recent examples from a world issue you have studied.

Describe question ?

International organisations that seek to resolve international issues and problems		
United Nations organisations	NATO	World Bank
European Union	African Union	Charities and other NGOs

Describe, **in detail**, **two** ways international organisations try to resolve an international issue or problem you have studied. **4 marks**

Hints & tips

*The international issue in this answer is **Development Issues in Africa**. You are expected to provide **examples** relevant to this issue. For this question you need to answer how international organisations have worked to resolve some of the issues that African countries face. You should pick two international organisations from the options – you will be able to choose from the African Union, UN organisations or charities and other NGOs using this study guide.*

Model answer

The work the UN does in developing nations in Africa is vital in supporting development. UNICEF works to improve and protect the lives of children in developing nations by trying to ensure all children receive their human rights. For example, UNICEF has built 415 new classrooms in the remotest parts of Mali and Burkina Faso so thousands of children can receive an education in the hope of a brighter future.

Many charities and non-governmental organisations (NGOs) also work to resolve issues in African nations. War Child specialises in helping children who have been affected by war. In Uganda thousands of children have suffered as child soldiers and War Child aims to help these children recover and live a normal life.

Marker's comment

The question requires that you clearly express how international organisations try to resolve an international issue and this answer describes how both UNICEF and NGOs aim to resolve development issues related to Africa. Up-to-date examples are included with reference to specific African nations. **4 marks**

Remember

In a describe question, up to 3 marks can be awarded for each description you give, depending on their quality, level of detail, relevance, accuracy and exemplification.

Explain question

Explain, **in detail**, **two** causes of an international issue or problem that you have studied. **6 marks**

Model answer

The first cause of underdevelopment among African countries is debt. Many African governments have borrowed money from the International Monetary Fund (IMF) or the World Bank to finance development. However, at times this money has been misspent and these institutions attach high interest rates to their loans that result in massive repayments for many years. This prevents countries spending enough money on education and health. In 2013, Angola's debt was over $18 billion.

The second cause of underdevelopment is armed conflict. Armed conflict can tear a country apart and have devastating effects on its social and economic development. Over the last few decades many African nations have been locked in civil war. Continuing conflict in Somalia has left the country in turmoil, with the south a highly dangerous place for civilians to live.

Marker's comment

This is a very good answer because it is relevant, makes accurate points with development, analysis and exemplification. Each paragraph clearly addresses a cause of underdevelopment like the question asks and provides examples. **6 marks**

Remember

Always structure your answers in paragraphs. Avoid list-type answers or bullet points.

Remember

In an explain question, up to 4 marks can be awarded for each explanation you make, depending on their quality, level of detail, relevance, accuracy and exemplification.

Hints & tips

Each knowledge and understanding question will ask you for either two or three explanations or descriptions. It is important to stick to the number the question asks for as you will lose marks if you write about fewer and may waste time if you write about more.

Also, look at how many marks the question is worth. Knowledge and understanding questions will be out of either 4, 6 or 8 marks. The amount you are expected to write for each answer depends on the number of marks. Use the point, explanation and example (P.E.E.) rule to help you achieve good marks.

Chapter 12

World Issues: International Terrorism

What you should know 

To be successful in this section, you should **know** and **understand**:

★ what the political, social and economic causes of terrorism are
★ the events of major terrorist attacks
★ the consequences of terrorism and how it has changed the world
★ links between human rights and terrorism
★ how the United Kingdom has responded to terrorism
★ how the international community has responded to terrorism
★ the successes and failures of an international organisation's response to terrorism.

The causes of terrorism

Terrorist attacks aim to achieve certain goals or are in retaliation for a particular event or policy. However, the causes of terrorism may overlap and a terrorist group may be active due to political, social and economic factors.

Political causes

Western foreign policy

Many of the high-profile terrorist attacks in Europe have been religiously motivated. However, as much as religion plays its part, those committing the attacks tend to be partly motivated and **radicalised** in reaction to the West's foreign policy. Islamic extremists want full removal of UK troops from the Middle East and an end to military action in which many thousands of innocent Muslims have been caught up.

Dictatorships and human rights violations

The democratic system in the UK means that every citizen has a voice. However, there are other countries that are run by **dictatorships**. These oppressive governments make decisions that are not fair for the majority of people in a country and as there are no elections the governments often remain in power for many years. Groups of citizens (commonly referred to as 'rebels') in countries like these may resort to terrorist activities to try and bring about political and social change within their country. As much as these groups may be engaging in 'terrorist activities' they may actually have widespread support among the population. The civil war in Syria is an example of this, as is the situation in Palestine and Israel.

Nationalism

In some countries or regions of the world there are people who want independence but feel they cannot achieve it peacefully. These people

Key words

Radicalisation: A process where a person or group increasingly adopts extreme political, social or religious views or ideas.
Dictatorship: A form of government in which a person or a small group rules with almost unlimited power.

therefore decide to turn to violence and terrorism to try and achieve their **nationalist** goals. These people are also sometimes referred to as 'separatists'. Separatist movements are surprisingly common around the world but few will take up arms in support of their cause. Palestinian terrorist groups have been waging a war with Israel over land for decades. These Palestinian terror groups do not recognise the state of Israel, and believe the land belongs to them and the nation of Palestine.

Key words

Nationalism: Nationalists believe that independence should be sought due to a common culture, heritage and language.

Sharia law: A set of principles that govern the moral and religious lives of Muslims.

Social and economic causes

Religion

Religion could also be regarded as a political cause of terrorism. It has been associated with terrorism for centuries. People who commit terrorist attacks in the name of their religion are referred to as 'religious extremists'. Islamic religious extremists were behind the 9/11 terrorist attacks, and indeed many of the terrorist attacks in the last decade. These extremists are upset by the West's involvement in affairs in the Middle East and believe the Western way of life to be very different from life in a Muslim country where society should be run according to an extreme form of **sharia law**. Islamic extremists are therefore waging a *jihad* (holy war) against the West and believe they are acting on behalf of their God to fulfil a duty. Islamic extremists believe that by carrying out terrorist attacks they become 'martyrs' and will be rewarded in the afterlife.

Poverty and deprivation

Terrorists may also be driven by a sense of deprivation and poverty within their society. This is currently happening in Somalia and Nigeria where many people have grown up in conditions of turmoil with a lack of education, prospects and employment. This has made individuals vulnerable to the arguments and promises of militant groups such as Boko Haram and al-Shabaab.

In an overlap with political causes, the government of a country suffering from terrorist activity within its borders may be corrupt and embezzling state funds. Therefore, the country will not have a functioning welfare state to support people or a successful economy to create jobs for its citizens. This can lead to young men and women joining terrorist groups that will sometimes pay them to be combatants. This has happened in Syria in recent years.

The impact and consequences of terrorism

'International terrorism' is the phrase now used to describe the many terror attacks that have occurred worldwide since 9/11. It brings home the idea that terrorism is now worldwide, not confined to countries in conflict.

Who is Islamic State (IS)?

Islamic State, often referred to as ISIS (Islamic State in Iraq and Syria), is an international terrorist organisation that has been active since 2014. It has carried out or claimed responsibility for numerous terror attacks in the Middle East, Europe and the US, some of which have resulted in dozens of innocent people dying.

Islamic State began as an off-shoot of al-Qaeda, the terrorist organisation responsible for the 9/11 attack in the US in 2001. IS has grown in size, wealth and power over recent years and is now considered the most dangerous terrorist group in the world.

IS – a history of violence

Attack	Year	Number killed
Barcelona van attack	2017	13
Manchester concert bombing	2017	23
Brussels bombings	2016	32
Berlin Christmas market attack	2016	12
Nice lorry attack	2016	86
Paris attacks	2015	130

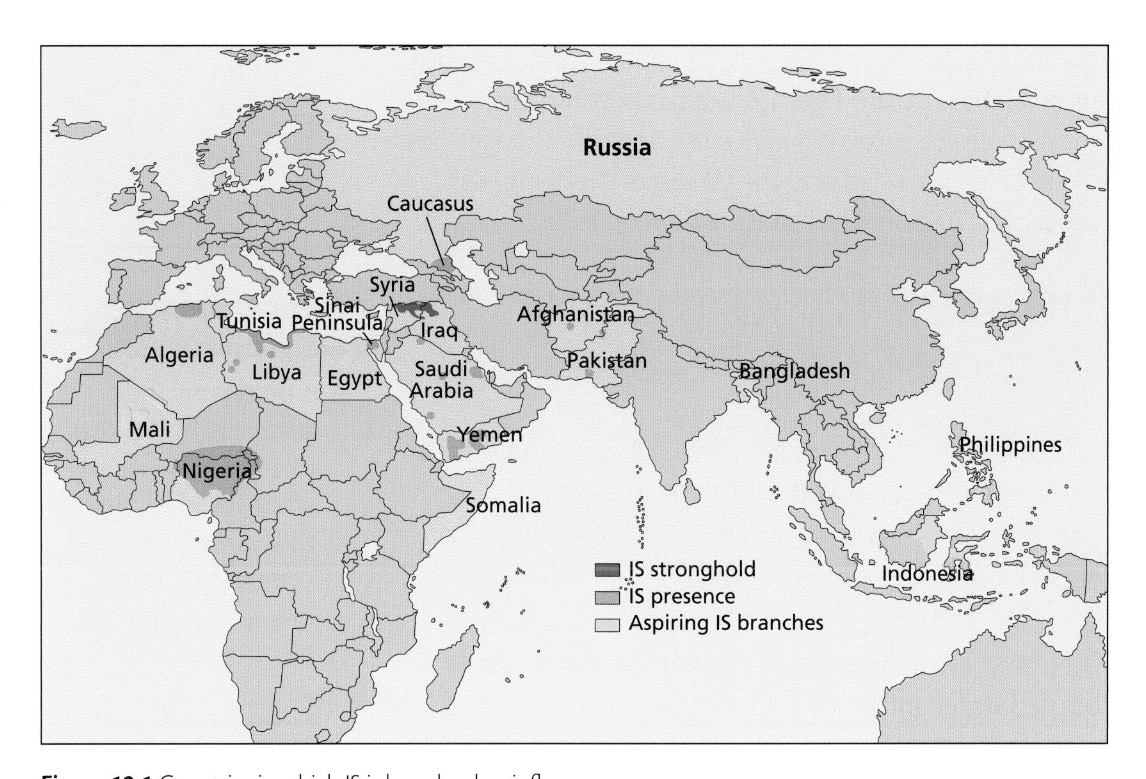

Figure 12.1 Countries in which IS is based or has influence

Major terror attacks

International terrorism has brought death, injury and fear in the form of terror attacks. In recent years, with the rise of IS, the number of terror attacks against the United Kingdom has increased. The following examples outline the devastation and destruction terrorism causes to citizens of the UK and France.

Manchester concert bombing

In May 2017, a suicide bomber blew himself up in the foyer of Manchester Arena as the audience left following a concert by US pop star Ariana Grande. The terrorist, Salman Abedi, was a 22-year-old UK-born citizen who had links to Libya and Islamic State. He was brought up in Manchester and had attended school in the city but is thought to have travelled to Syria where he became radicalised. The attack killed 22 people, mainly children and teenagers, and injured over 100 more.

Paris attacks

The attacks in Paris on the night of Friday 13 November 2015 by IS gunmen and suicide bombers hit a concert hall, a major stadium, restaurants and bars, almost simultaneously – and left 130 people dead and hundreds wounded. The deadliest scene of the co-ordinated attack was at the Bataclan Concert Hall where three attackers wearing suicide belts stormed into the back of the concert hall. The men fired automatic assault rifles into the crowd, killing 89 people. They then killed themselves by blowing up their vests after a shoot-out with police.

> **Hints & tips**
>
> *When answering an exam question on the consequences of an international issue like terrorism it is important that you know some of the major terrorist attacks to use as examples.*

Trouble in North Africa

Although the threat of terrorism has traditionally come from countries like Afghanistan and Pakistan, there is now more terrorist activity in North Africa. Countries like Somalia and Mali are becoming popular with terrorists because of the lack of policing and infrastructure. North Africa has become a major focus for counter-terrorism efforts, particularly since the Algerian hostage crisis in early 2013 where 38 people were killed, and the Westgate shopping mall attack in Kenya, in September 2013, in which at least 72 people died.

Consequences for ordinary citizens

Since 9/11 the world has changed dramatically. The USA and Britain are at war in the Middle East, supporting the **war on terror**. Western governments have increased security measures to reduce the threat to their countries. The Western population now lives with the risk of terrorism in their everyday lives.

> **Key words**
>
> **War on terror**: The general name for the international military effort spearheaded by the US and the UK to combat terrorism.

Security has been increased at UK airports. Before 9/11 air passengers were able to take bottled water and items such as scissors in their hand luggage but this is now forbidden. There are also stricter security systems to pass through, for example London Heathrow Airport uses a biometrics system to scan passengers' eyes and check them against a database. There are also more armed police in the departure areas.

Islamophobia

Within Western societies there has been an increase in 'Islamophobia' – the dislike or irrational fear of Muslims. After a jihadist terror attack, such as in London in 2017, violence against ordinary Muslims increases. After the Manchester concert bombing in June 2017, hate crimes against Muslims increased by 500% in the city.

How does terrorism impact on the human rights of civilians around the world?

Human rights are universal rights to which everyone is entitled. In 1948, after the Second World War, the United Nations drew up a list of basic rights that all humans should have. These rights can be found in the 1948 Universal Declaration of Human Rights. (See page 112 for a list of some of these universal rights.)

Terrorism hopes to destroy human rights, destabilise governments and spread fear throughout countries. It aims to reduce people's feelings of security and prevent them from enjoying some human rights, including the rights to life and liberty. Everyone should be entitled to live their life peacefully without the threat or fear from terrorist crimes such as bombings, murder, intimidation or kidnapping.

Human rights in Afghanistan

Before 2001, Afghanistan was ruled by the Taliban, who ran the country using an extreme form of sharia law. The citizens of Afghanistan, especially women, had very few human rights. Under this system women had to be covered from head to toe and were not allowed to work, play sports or wear make-up.

The USA led an invasion into Afghanistan in 2001 and since then progress has been made on human rights. The country is now controlled by a democratic government. But human rights in Afghanistan are still poor compared to Scotland. The Taliban is still present in many areas of the country and works against the decisions of the Government.

Figure 12.2 Malala Yousafzai, a Pakistani schoolgirl who challenged the Taliban ban on female education, was shot in the head by gunmen who stopped her school bus and asked for her by name. Taliban militants specifically targeted Malala for her work in encouraging women's education and rights. Malala survived her attack and is recovering after being flown to the UK for specialised medical treatment. In 2013 she addressed the UN General Assembly and was nominated for the Nobel Peace Prize.

How has the UK responded to international terrorism?

UK military response

The war on terror began in 2001 with the invasion of Afghanistan in search of Osama bin Laden, leader of al-Qaeda. The UK continues to have troops deployed to various countries in the Middle East, including Afghanistan, Syria and Iraq, but not in a combat role. The main priority for the UK now is defeating IS and this work is being done as part of a Global Coalition. The UK military plays a leading role in the Global Coalition through committing military personnel to help train Iraqi soldiers in engineering, medical skills and basic infantry. Although the UK has not committed soldiers to help fighting on the ground, the Royal Air Force has conducted over 1500 airstrikes in Iraq and Syria – more than any other Coalition country bar America – and provides highly advanced intelligence and surveillance to Iraqi Security Forces. UK military action has been successful in killing many IS fighters as well as winning back territory controlled by the terror group.

See the drones case study (page 125) for further information about the UK military response.

Counter-terrorism

The UK Government's counter-terrorism strategy is called 'CONTEST' and has four main aims:

1. The Government will work to *pursue* terrorists and disrupt their work.
2. They will *prevent* terrorism by countering the various factors that cause people to become terrorists.
3. The Government will work to *protect* the public through increased vigilance and security.
4. Lastly, they will *prepare for* and minimise the potential harm caused by terrorist attacks if they do occur.

The Scottish Government works within this strategy and operates its own special counter-terrorism unit called the 'Scottish Preventing Violent Extremism Unit'.

The role of the police

The threat of terrorism has changed the role of police in our society. Police forces now train officers specifically in counter-terrorism. Police also track 'online terrorist activity', known as cyber-terrorism, and are able to watch over the internet for people using cyberspace to promote, glorify or help carry out acts of terrorism and violent extremism.

How has the international community responded to terrorism?

The USA

Since 9/11, America has led the fight against international terrorism and is currently involved in many efforts to combat terrorism including the Global Coalition with the UK. The US is primarily involved in Syria where it has deployed troops to fight against ISIS. It has also conducted over 8000 airstrikes in the country. However, the US is still involved in Afghanistan as well, where thousands of troops remain trying to stabilise the country and defeat the Taliban. The war in Afghanistan is the longest war in which America has ever been involved.

Drone attacks – the US and the UK military response

The US and the UK have increasingly used 'unmanned aerial vehicles', known commonly as drones, to target terrorists living in remote areas in countries such as Pakistan, Afghanistan and Syria. Drones have multiple uses such as gathering intelligence through surveillance, listening to mobile phone conversations and actively attacking suspected terrorists. However, the use of drones has been criticised as drones have killed hundreds of innocent people in the hunt for suspected terrorists. It is this sort of tactic employed by the US and UK that is said to fuel terrorism.

Trump's Muslim travel ban

In 2017 US President Donald Trump banned immigrants and refugees from six mainly Muslim countries from entering the USA. Unless they have a clear relationship with America – either through family, schools or a job – visitors from Iran, Libya, Somalia, Sudan, Syria and Yemen are banned. Trump believes the ban will protect the USA from potentially dangerous individuals and make it a safer place.

The death of Osama bin Laden

In May 2011, US special forces found and killed Osama bin Laden, leader of al-Qaeda and the mastermind behind the 9/11 terrorist attacks, who had been living in Pakistan. This was a major breakthrough for the USA and the international community in the fight against terrorism. Bin Laden was not only the head of al-Qaeda but he was seen by extremists around the world as the leader in the fight against the West.

Figure 12.3 Osama bin Laden

The response of international organisations to terrorism

Two important international organisations that help to prevent and stop terrorist attacks on their members are the United Nations (UN) and the North Atlantic Treaty Organization (NATO).

The United Nations

Countries joining the UN agree to work together to maintain peace and security in the world. Through the UN the international community has agreed on a global strategy to combat terrorism.

Figure 12.4 Aims of the UN Global Strategy against Terrorism

North Atlantic Treaty Organization (NATO)

NATO is made up of 28 countries that have a military and political alliance with each other. It was created after the Second World War to help prevent any future wars.

NATO assists worldwide in the fight against terrorism. A key aspect to its function and aims is cooperation between member states on terror-related issues, such as sharing intelligence. NATO also works to stabilise regions following conflict such as leading the International Security Assistance Force (ISAF) that is helping the Afghan Government to create a stable nation. This includes creating a political system with free and fair elections as well as training the Afghan police and military to ensure the rule of law in society. As of 2018 there are around 15,000 NATO troops in Afghanistan.

The European Union

The European Union works to reduce the threat of terrorism in EU countries. Cooperation between states is vital, as is the sharing of terrorist-related intelligence. When a terrorist attack happens in an EU country, other member nations come to their aid. In addition, Europol (the European law enforcement agency) works to make Europe safer by helping the member nations of the European Union in the fight against serious international crime and terrorism.

The successes and failures of an international organisation in responding to terrorism

Since 9/11 in 2001, terrorist activity around the globe has increased dramatically. The Global Terrorism Index of 2017 shows IS is officially the deadliest terrorist group in the world, claiming responsibility for 6141 deaths through attacks in more than 250 cities in 2016. It can therefore easily be argued that no one organisation (or nation) has been successful in tackling the issue of international terrorism.

The European Union

The EU has had some success in tackling terrorism. Europol's 2017 Terrorism Situation and Trend Report states that the EU made 1002 arrests for terrorist offences (such as preparing, financing, assisting, attempting or executing attacks) and 77 arrests for travelling to conflict zones for terrorist purposes. Importantly, they also managed to foil 142 attacks, half of which were due to take place in the UK.

However, the fact remains that in 2016 and 2017 the EU suffered numerous deadly terrorist attacks in various countries. The UK, France and Germany all suffered attacks from both right-wing terrorists as well as jihadist terrorists. Those who carried out the deadliest attacks in Paris in 2016 freely moved between Belgium and France and had also managed to fly to Syria. The open border policy between EU countries as well as the limited intelligence-sharing between member states has allowed terrorists to attack at will. Countries of the EU often have their own methods, policies and ideas for tackling terrorism which take priority over working as part of the Union.

Questions and model answers

Hints & tips

The international issue of focus for you is ***International Terrorism****. You are expected to provide* ***examples*** *relevant to this issue. For this question you need to answer how international organisations have worked to resolve some of the issues that terrorism causes. You should aim to pick two international organisations from the options – you will be able to choose from the United Nations, NATO or the European Union using this study guide.*

Remember

Knowledge and understanding questions will have 4, 6 or 8 marks allocated and you will need to answer two or three questions 'describing' or 'explaining'. You must give recent examples from a world issue you have studied.

Describe question

International organisations that aim to resolve international issues and problems		
United Nations organisations	NATO	World Bank
European Union	African Union	Charities and other NGOs

Describe, **in detail**, **two** ways in which international organisations try to resolve an international issue or problem you have studied. **4 marks**

Model answer

International organisations work hard to respond to issues that have a negative impact on people around the world. Firstly, the North Atlantic Treaty Organization (NATO) has responded to terrorism by assisting with the fight against terrorism in Afghanistan. NATO is helping to rebuild the nation and is working on training the Afghan military and police service. NATO also has a response force to deal rapidly with any attacks on member states.

Secondly, the European Union (EU) has responded to terrorism by increasing cooperation between member states. For example, when terrorists targeted Paris in 2016, other EU nations worked to assist to find out who was responsible. Also, Europol – the European law enforcement agency – carries out investigations and gathers intelligence about suspected terrorist activity in and around Europe and shares it with member nations.

Marker's comment

This is a very good answer because it is relevant and makes accurate points with development, analysis and exemplification. Each paragraph clearly addresses an attempt at resolution by an international organisation like the question asks and provides examples. This answer doesn't need to be of great length as it is only worth 4 marks. This answer would achieve 4/4. **4 marks**

> **Remember**
>
> Always structure your answers in paragraphs. Avoid list-type answers or bullet points.

Explain question

Explain, **in detail**, **three** socio-economic causes of an international issue or problem you have studied. **8 marks**

> **Hints & tips**
>
> 
>
> *Look at how many marks the question is worth. Knowledge and understanding questions will be out of either 4, 6 or 8 marks. The amount you are expected to write for each answer depends on the number of marks. Work with the idea that a paragraph is worth at least 2 marks if you include a **point**, **explanation** and **example** (P.E.E.).*

Model answer

There are various socio-economic causes of terrorism. A group may resort to terrorism due to religious extremism. Muslim extremists strongly disagree with the Western way of life and would prefer to control countries under an extreme version of sharia law. IS, which eventually wants to create a worldwide Islamic state, has carried out terrorist attacks against Western countries for this reason, including the Manchester Arena attack of 2017.

Other socio-economic reasons can also be considered causes of terrorism. If a particular group within a country faces discrimination from the the majority of people or the Government then they may resort to terrorism in retaliation. It can be argued that some Muslims may have been motivated to become radicalised due to facing discrimination in or by Western countries.

⇨

Similarly, poverty can be regarded as a cause of terrorism. Having no prospects in terms of education and employment, especially in poorer developing countries, can lead to higher rates of radicalisation. In Somalia, growing up in conditions of conflict and deprivation has made many Somalis vulnerable to the arguments and promises of terrorist group al-Shabaab.

Marker's comment

This is an 8-mark question so requires a response of good length and depth. The answer clearly outlines the main socio-economic causes of terrorism and for each gives relevant, up-to-date examples. In each paragraph there is analysis and a clear explanation of each cause of terrorism – as required by the question. The point, explain, example structure is apparent to see, which is a useful way to ensure that answers pick up good marks.

This answer would easily achieve full marks. **8 marks**

Part Five: Source-based questions

There are three types of skills questions and you will have practised these in your classwork. The three source-based skills are as follows:

- Using sources of information to support and oppose a point of view.
- Using sources of information to make and justify a decision.
- Using sources of information to draw and support conclusions.

Your teacher may also use National 5 unit assessments for practice, but these do not form part of your examined content.

Remember

In your course exam the source-based questions can appear in any of the three Sections, so using sources of information to make and justify a decision could be a question in the International Issues section of the exam.

All questions that assess the evaluation of sources will be allocated 10 marks.

To achieve full marks, you must refer to all sources in your answer.

You can gain a maximum of 3 marks for each well-developed point you make, depending on the quality of argument and accurate use of evidence.

Chapter 13
Democracy in Scotland and the UK

Democracy in Scotland

The following shows an example of how to use sources of information to support and oppose views.

Skills question 

Study Sources 1, 2 and 3 and then answer the question that follows.

You have been asked to recommend who should be your party's candidate in the local council elections in Linburn.

Option 1	Option 2
Candidate Lucas Watt	Candidate Sophie Willis

Source 1 Candidates' statements

Lucas Watt: secondary school teacher, age 44

I support the housing development as in the long run it will provide new facilities for Linburn and will bring in more council tax. This development will provide lots of jobs for the area and should be supported. The creation of a new industrial estate will provide employment opportunities for all.

With severe cuts to local authorities' budgets continuing to be made, we must try to increase our revenue. As such, I support an increase in council tax to protect local services. It has remained frozen for many years.

We have a low crime rate and we cannot justify the reopening of the police station. Police Scotland has to make severe cuts to its budget. We should set up Neighbourhood Watch networks to protect our community.

Many parents are concerned about the future education of their children. The influx of young families to the area could lead to the local primary school having too many pupils and having to turn pupils away. So I support the immediate building of a second primary school and, within six years, an expansion to our secondary school.

Sophie Willis: health worker, age 46

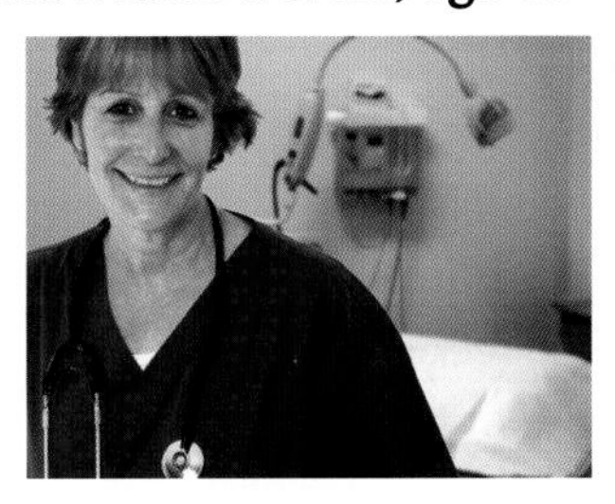

I am against any increase in council tax as it will hit hard on those in work and on most of our elderly. Our residents face severe pressure on family budgets and the last thing we need is an increase in council tax.

Our most urgent priority is health provision rather than education. Many of our elderly residents are concerned that the local health centre will soon not be able to meet their health needs. As such I support the immediate building of a second health centre. Our schools can easily cope with the increase in demand and so are not a priority.

I support only a limited housing programme so that we can monitor its effects on Linburn. We already have major parking problems and traffic jams at peak times which create frustration and accidents. I support an improvement in our transport links to manage the increased volume of traffic.

Crime is a major concern in the area and this is reflected in the findings of our Community Council. I will fight for the restoration of our police station. Our elderly population need better protection – they do not feel safe even during the day.

Source 2

Linburn is a council area in the West of Scotland with a population of about 6000. It is an established community with over 80% of its residents owning their own homes. Some are concerned that council tax might be raised; others would accept an increase if it means no cuts to education and community health budgets. A new massive private housing development is being built in Linburn which will eventually double the population.

The local secondary school has a very good reputation and standards are high. However, residents are concerned that the present health and educational services will not be able to cope with the increase in population. There are plans to eventually provide a new primary school, community centre and leisure centre. An industrial site is already being built to attract small firms to the area which will improve the local economy.

Linburn is only five miles from the nearest town, which has one of the highest crime rates in the country. Many Linburn residents are concerned about the growing crime rate, especially the elderly. Frank Clark, chair of the Community Council stated, 'More and more residents are contacting me about attempted and actual house break-ins, we need a stronger police presence'.

Profile of Linburn – key statistics (%)

	Linburn	Scotland
Number of pensioners	13	10
Home ownership	82	67
Unemployed and seeking work	5	7
School leavers – 3 or more Highers	40	30
Experiencing long-term poor health	20	18

Source 3

Survey of public opinion in Linburn

	Strongly agree (%)	Agree (%)	Disagree (%)	Strongly disagree (%)
Crime is a growing problem in Linburn	21	28	30	21
Council tax needs to be increased	20	25	35	20
The housing development is good for Linburn	16	38	32	14
The priority for Linburn is a second health centre and a new primary school	18	40	32	10

You must decide which option to recommend, **either** Lucas Watt (Option 1) **or** Sophie Willis (Option 2).

(i) Using Sources 1, 2 and 3, **which option would you choose**?
(ii) Give reasons to **support** your choice.
(iii) **Explain** why you did not choose the other option.

Your answer **must** be based on all three sources. **10 marks**

Remember

A justifying a decision (options) question is worth 10 marks in the question paper.

It is not the case that one option is correct and the other is incorrect; either can be chosen for full marks as evidence is contained within the sources to allow you to justify either decision or recommendation.

For full marks you must also explain why you have rejected the other option. An answer that deals with only one option will be awarded a maximum of 8 marks.

To achieve full marks, all sources must be used and you must show evidence that supports the view as well as evidence that opposes the view.

Model answers

Option 1: Recommend Lucas Watt

I would recommend Lucas Watt because he is a school teacher with experience in education (Source 1).

Lucas Watt states that parents are concerned about the future education of their children (Source 1). The population is going to double with the building of a massive number of private homes (Source 2) and his proposal to begin building a new primary school is sound. This is backed up in Source 3 which shows that a clear majority regard the building of a new primary school as a priority.

We should also support Lucas Watt because he supports the housing development which will provide new facilities for Linburn and provide jobs for the area (Source 1). This is backed up in Source 2 which shows that a community centre and leisure centre will be built and this will greatly improve the local amenities. An industrial site is being built already.

Reason for rejecting other option:

I rejected Option 2 because Sophie Willis is against the housing development (Source 1). However, in Source 3 the local opinion poll clearly shows that the majority state that the housing development is good for Linburn.

Sophie Willis states that the schools can easily cope with the increase in demand (Source 1). However, the population is going to double and residents are concerned that educational services will not be able to cope (Source 2).This is backed up in Source 1 as the influx of young families could lead to pupils being turned away.

⇨

Option 2: Recommend Sophie Willis

I would recommend Sophie Willis because she is a health worker with experience in health provision (Source 1).

Sophie Willis also states in Source 1 that she is against an increase in council tax as it will hit those in work and the elderly hard. Source 3 shows that in the survey of public opinion a clear majority are against an increase in rates.

We should also support Sophie Willis as she states that the most urgent priority is health provision and she supports the immediate building of a second health service. This is backed up in Source 2 which highlights that Linburn has above the national average of people experiencing long-term poor health (20% to 18% national average). The fact that the population will also double puts further strain on health provision.

Finally I would recommend Sophie Willis as she states that crime is a major concern in the area and she wants the police station reopened. Source 2 backs this up as many residents, especially the elderly, are concerned about the growing crime rate.

Reason for rejecting other option:

I rejected Option 1 because Lucas Watt is against the reopening of the police station. Although crime is low (Source 1), Linburn is only five miles away from a town that has one of the highest crime rates in the country and so local people are concerned, especially the elderly. The Community Council argue that Linburn needs a stronger police presence (Source 2).

Marker's comment

Both answers are very well structured and make use of five paragraphs. The option chosen is clearly stated at the beginning of both answers. Both answers make reference to all three sources.

Every paragraph in each of the two answers shows interaction between two sources. Evidence is accurate, detailed and relevant, with justification that is linked between two sources. Also, each answer includes a reason why the other option was rejected, with accurate, detailed and relevant justification that is also linked between two sources.

So, overall two very good, high-quality answers regardless of which option is chosen, and both deserving of full marks. **10 marks**

Chapter 14

Social Issues in the UK

Social inequality

The following shows an example of how to use sources of information to support and oppose a point of view.

Skills question 

Study Sources 1, 2 and 3 and then answer the question that follows.

Source 1

Facts and viewpoints about zero-hours contracts

A zero-hours contract is a form of employment contract under which an employer does not have to state how many hours the employee will work per week. This means employees work only when they are needed by their employer. They will only be paid for the hours they work. So on one particular week the employee may only work 15 hours but 30 hours the following week.

This type of work contract is being used increasingly by UK employers. In 2015 the figure stood at an estimated 900,000 compared to 650,000 in 2013.

Well-known companies such as McDonald's and Sports Direct use these contracts as do the NHS and charities. Zero-hours contracts are higher among young people than other age groups with 37% of those employed on such contracts aged between 16 and 24.

Viewpoint of Michelle Kelly: retired clerical assistant

Although retired, I am working part time on a zero-hours contract which gives me flexibility and keeps me active. I can spend time with my grandchildren and the income I receive allows me to have a better standard of living. I work alongside some university students who can combine their studies with some work and income. My employer is happy with this arrangement, and I am in control of my work–life balance. So I am happy to have a zero-hours contract.

Viewpoint of Sam Gunn: hotel worker

I am on a zero-hours contract and I feel I am being exploited by my employer. My contract effectively stops me from taking a second job even if I am down for only ten hours for the coming week as my contract states that I must be available at all times. These contracts mean employers avoid redundancy pay and pension contributions. I would prefer guaranteed weekly hours so that I can plan my finances. Some months I have to use food banks and take out payday loans with very high interest rates.

Source 2

Survey findings of employment satisfaction – zero-hour and non zero-hour workers (2014)

	Zero-hours contract	Non zero-hours contract
Satisfied with job	50%	57%
Work–life balance	65%	58%
Prefer more hours	45%	10%

Source 3

Gross weekly pay and average hours per week (zero-hours and non zero-hours workers)

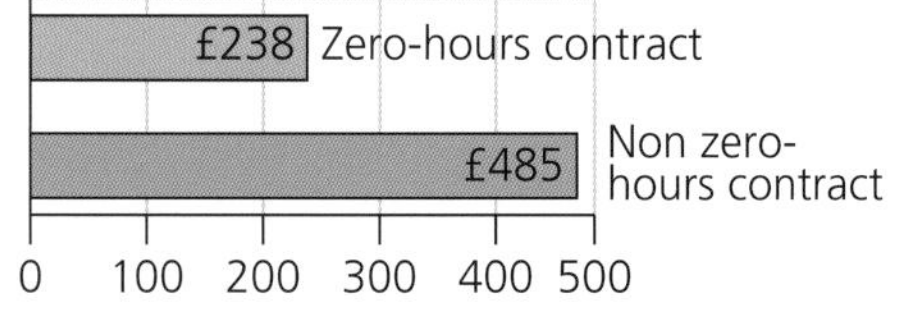

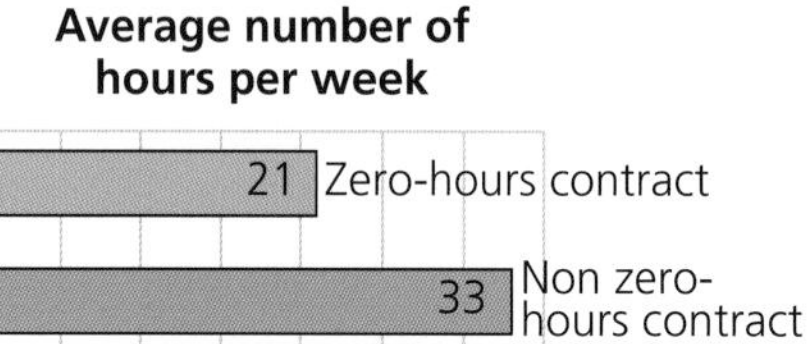

Using Sources 1, 2 and 3, explain why the view of **Ryan Willis is selective in the use of facts**.

> Zero-hours contract workers are exploited by their employers.
>
> View of Ryan Willis

In your answer you must:

- give evidence from the sources that support Ryan Willis' view
  and
- give evidence from the sources that oppose Ryan Willis' view.

Your answer must be based on all **three** sources. **10 marks**

Remember

Remember that when answering this question the marker is looking for you to be able to evaluate a limited range of sources, **detecting** and **explaining** instances of supporting and opposing a point of view giving developed **arguments**.

Up to 3 marks will be awarded for a developed explanation, depending upon the quality of argument and accurate use of evidence.

If you only give evidence to *either* support or oppose the viewpoint you can only be awarded a maximum of 6 marks. To achieve full marks *all* sources must be used and you must also provide evidence that supports the view, as well as evidence that opposes the view.

Model answers

Evidence to support the viewpoint:

Sam Gunn in Source 1 feels that he is being exploited by his employers as he is not guaranteed set weekly hours so sometimes he has to use food banks as he does not have enough money. Over 40% of those on zero-hours contracts want more working hours compared to only 10% of workers on set contracts (Source 2). This highlights their lack of working hours.

Source 1 also highlights that zero-hours employees only work when they are needed by their employer and this can impact on income. Gross weekly pay for these workers is less than half compared to non zero-hours contracts (Source 3). This highlights the massive difference in income.

Evidence to oppose the viewpoint:

Source 1 highlights that many workers are happy to have zero-hours contracts as it gives flexibility. Retired Michelle Kelly enjoys her contract as it brings in extra money and she still has time to see her grandchildren, so she does not feel exploited.

Source 1 also highlights that zero-hours contracts suit students who can combine their studies with earning money. This is supported in the survey of employment satisfaction where more people on these contracts feel they have the correct work–life balance (65% compared to 58% on non zero-hours workers).

Marker's comment

This is an excellent answer as it displays integration of sources with appropriate evaluative comments. All sources are used with detailed evidence used to support and oppose the viewpoint. The candidate's evidence to support the viewpoint is outstanding as both paragraphs integrate two sources to provide evaluative comments. The candidate attempts to evaluate the source by using phrases such as 'highlights the massive difference in income' and 'does not feel exploited'. **10 marks**

Crime and the law

The following shows an example of how to use sources of information to make and justify a decision.

Skills question 

Study Sources 1, 2 and 3 and then answer the question that follows.

Source 1

Facts and viewpoints on the use of taser guns

A taser or stun gun uses compressed air to fire two darts that trail electric cables back to the handset. When the dart strikes, a five-second 50,000-volt charge is released that causes the suspect's muscles to contract uncontrollably.

Police officers who are issued with taser guns go on a three-day training course. All of these officers are properly trained. Any use of a taser must be recorded and its use justified.

An officer can point a taser gun at an individual which creates a red dot. This usually leads to the individual ending their aggressive behaviour.

A police official stated: 'I know it is controversial, but tasers are an effective and non-lethal way of stopping a criminal in their tracks'. However, innocent people can be tasered.

The youngest person a taser gun was used on in the UK was a 14-year-old boy. In the USA over 300 people have died after being tasered.

In 2014, 10,400 incidents were logged of police having a taser gun. However, they were only used in 20% of the incidents. The availability of taser guns may damage the trust that exists between the police and UK citizens.

Source 2

The debate over the use of tasers

I was stabbed with a ten-inch butcher's knife while on duty and required extensive surgery.

I was off work for six months and I still have nightmares about what happened. I could easily have died and left my three children without a father. If I had a taser gun, I could have protected myself and the public. I could easily have disarmed the criminal. Violent crime is rising and the life of a police officer is becoming more dangerous.

Viewpoint of a London Police Officer

The increase in the use of taser guns is of major concern. Taser guns are a danger to the public and evidence from the USA supports this claim. Taser guns are widely used in the USA. In recent years several men have died in England after being tasered. Mistakes can also be made by the police, for example, in 2012 a police officer tasered a blind man. The police officer thought that his white cane was a Samurai sword!

Viewpoint of a human rights supporter

Source 3

Public opinion survey on the use of tasers by the police (% agreeing with statement)

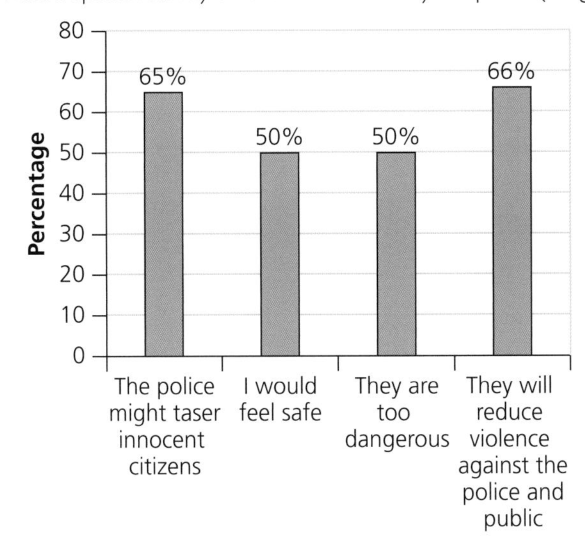

Using Sources 1, 2 and 3, explain why the view of Catherine Daly is selective in the use of facts.

> The use of taser guns is a danger to all.
>
> Catherine Daly

In your answer you must:

- give evidence from the sources that support Catherine Daly's view

  and

- give evidence from the sources that oppose Catherine Daly's view.

Your answer must be based on all **three** sources. **10 marks**

Remember

Remember that when answering this question the marker is looking for you to be able to evaluate a limited range of sources, **detecting** and **explaining** instances of supporting and opposing a point of view giving developed **arguments**.

Up to 3 marks will be awarded for a developed explanation depending upon the quality of argument and accurate use of evidence.

If you only give evidence to *either* support *or* oppose the viewpoint you can only be awarded a maximum of 6 marks.

To achieve full marks, *all* sources must be used and you must also provide evidence that supports the view as well as evidence that opposes the view.

Model answer

Evidence to support the viewpoint:

The human rights supporter in Source 2 argues that taser guns are a danger to the public and refers to evidence of the seriously high number of taser deaths in the USA. This is supported in Source 1 which states that innocent people can be injured. For example, a blind man was tasered after the police officer thought he was carrying a dangerous weapon. This shows that the use of tasers is a danger to the public.

Source 2 states that the use of taser guns is of major concern. This concern is reflected in Source 3 with a large majority of those interviewed agreeing that the police might taser innocent citizens. This clearly shows that they are aware that taser guns can be a danger to the general public.

Evidence to oppose the viewpoint:

Source 2 highlights that a police officer in London is convinced that the use of taser guns protects not just the police but the public as well. This is supported in the survey on the police use of tasers with two-thirds of the public agreeing that their use will reduce violence against the police and public (Source 3). So they are a protection not a threat.

Catherine is also wrong as having a taser gun may defuse a dangerous situation with the 'individual ending their aggressive behaviour'. In 2014, the police had to use a taser gun in only one out of five incidents (Source 1). This shows that taser guns deter violent crime and protect the public. A policeman argues that he would not have been seriously wounded if he had had a taser gun (Source 2).

Marker's comment

This is an excellent answers as it displays integration of sources with appropriate evaluative comments. All sources are used with detailed evidence used to support and oppose the viewpoint. The candidate's evidence to support the viewpoint is outstanding as both paragraphs integrate two sources to provide evaluative comments. The candidate attempts to evaluate the source by using phrases such as 'So they are a protection not a threat' and 'major concern'. **10 marks**

Chapter 15
International Issues

World powers

The following shows an example of how to use sources of information to draw and support conclusions.

Remember

The country referred to in the skills question will be one of the G7 countries you have studied *or* one of the following: Brazil, China, India, Russia, South Africa *or* an 'enhanced reality' scenario.

Remember also that conclusion questions are worth 10 marks and that for full marks you must use all the sources and give four developed conclusions.

Remember

It is good practice to use the bullet points as headings before using the sources or evidence to draw conclusions. Another good approach is to put your conclusion at the start or the end of the evidence. It is very important that you come to a conclusion about each statement, rather than simply writing out large pieces of sources without coming to a relevant conclusion.

Remember that when answering this question you must identify the correct conclusion for each of the four statements and provide evidence from across the sources. Your answer will be highly credited if you draw conclusions which show interaction between the sources.

Skills question ?

Study Sources 1, 2 and 3 and then answer the question that follows.

Source 1

USA presidential elections

Elections for president are held every four years. President Obama, the Democratic Party candidate, won his first presidential election in 2008 and was re-elected in 2012.

The president of the USA is not chosen directly by the US people. The electoral college elects the president. Each state receives a set number of electoral college votes depending on its population size. For example, Florida, with a large population, receives 29 electoral college votes compared to the 3 received by Vermont which has a small population.

There are 538 electoral college votes in total. Citizens in each state vote for their respective presidential candidates. The candidate with the most votes in say, Florida, wins all of the electoral college votes of that state.

In 2008, the Democratic candidate Barack Obama made history by becoming the first African-American president of the USA. Obama secured victory with the highest ever recorded popular votes (the total number of votes received across the 50 states). Obama received over 66 million popular votes and he received 365 votes in the electoral college.

In the 2012 presidential election, Obama was re-elected president. He received over 65 million votes compared to the Republican candidate, Mick Romney, who won 61 million votes. In the electoral college, Obama won 332 votes compared to the Republican candidate who won 206.

In the 2012 election, the young, poorer groups and those from an ethnic minority background tended to support Obama, while older and white voters tended to favour the Republican candidate.

Source 2

US presidential election results 2012 and 2008

Party and candidate	Popular vote 2012	Popular vote 2008
Democrats: Obama	51.0%	52.9%
Republican: Romney	47.1%	45.6%

Party and candidate	Electoral college votes 2012	Electoral college votes 2008
Democrats: Obama	61.7%	67.8%
Republican: Romney	38.3%	32.2%

Source 3

Voting in 2012 presidential election by age and ethnicity

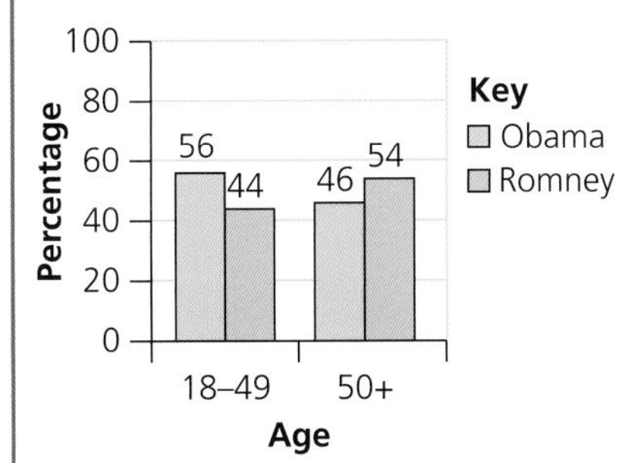

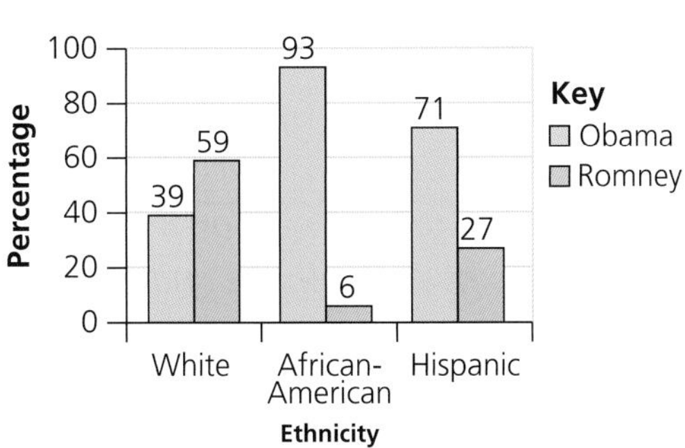

Using Sources 1, 2 and 3, what **conclusions** can be drawn about the 2012 USA presidential election?

You should reach a conclusion about **each** of the following:

- the electoral college results of 2012 compared to 2008
- the popular vote results of 2012 compared to 2008
- the link between age and voting behaviour in the 2012 election
- the link between ethnicity and voting behaviour in the 2012 election.

Your conclusions **must** be supported by evidence from the sources. You should link information within and between the sources in support of your conclusions.

Your answer must be based on all **three** sources. **10 marks**

Model answer

The electoral college results of 2012 compared to 2008

The conclusion is that in both elections Obama had a clear majority of the electoral college votes, but in the 2012 election the Republicans had increased their support and narrowed the difference.

This is supported in Sources 1 and 2. In 2008 Obama received 365 votes, almost 70%, with the Republican candidate winning less than a third of the votes. However, in the 2012 election the Republican candidate increased his votes to 206 with Obama winning about 62% of the votes.

The popular results of 2012 compared to 2008

The conclusion is that in both elections Obama had a clear majority of the popular votes but in the 2012 election the Republicans had increased their support and narrowed the difference.

This is supported in Sources 1 and 2. In 2008 Obama received 66 million votes, the highest ever recorded popular vote. However, in 2012 this declined to 65 million votes with the Republican candidate increasing his party's share of the votes from just under 46% to 47%. Obama's percentage of the votes fell by almost 2%.

The link between age and voting behaviour in the 2012 election

The elderly were more likely to vote for the Republican candidate and the young more likely to vote for Obama.

This is supported in Source 1 which states that young voters tended to support Obama and older voters Romney. Source 3 highlights this age divide. Those over the age of 50 favoured Romney with an 8-point difference. In contrast, Obama had a 12-point lead with the under-50 age group.

The link between ethnicity and voting behaviour in the 2012 election

White people were more likely to vote for the Republican candidate and ethnic minorities were more likely to vote for Obama.

This is supported in Source 1 which states that ethnic minority voters tended to support Obama and white voters Romney. Source 3 highlights this race divide. White voters favoured Romney with a 20-point difference. In contrast, Obama had a staggering 93% of African-American support.

Marker's comment

This is an excellent answer and is well structured. The candidate makes an original conclusion at the beginning of each paragraph and uses two sources to back up each of the four conclusions. All three sources are used over the course of the answer. Clear linkage between the sources has been made which demonstrates a high level of aptitude in answering this type of question.

Each of the candidate's paragraphs is worth 3 marks but as the maximum mark is 10, the full 10 marks are given. **10 marks**

Remember

- You must make an original conclusion.
- You should use more than one source to support each original conclusion.
- Use all three sources in your answer.
- For full marks, four developed conclusions must be given.

World issues

The following shows an example of how to use sources of information to draw and support conclusions.

Skills question 

Study Sources 1, 2 and 3 and then answer the question that follows.

Source 1

Progress in development and aid

In September 2015, the United Nations held a special conference to unveil the Sustainable Development Goals (SDGs) that will shape aid and development for the next 15 years. The conference was attended by the largest gathering ever of world leaders and donors such as Bill Gates. The new SDGs replace the previous Millennium Development Goals (MDGs) which have mostly been achieved largely because of progress in China and India.

However, one area that has been disappointing is the failure of the wealthiest countries to honour their promise to increase their spending on development aid. Of the leading nations only the United Kingdom has reached the agreed goal of spending 0.7 per cent of their gross domestic income (GDI). The USA would argue that they spend $33 billion a year on foreign aid which is the highest for any country (the UK spends $19 million). However, given the massive wealth of the USA this is an insignificant amount of their GDP.

One area of progress is in the determination of the international community, with support from wealthy donors such as Bill Gates, to tackle the killer diseases of malaria and HIV/AIDS. Africa has the highest number of those infected by these diseases. Of the 34 million world citizens who have AIDS, a staggering 24 million live in Africa. In 2014 an estimated 90% of those who died from malaria worldwide lived in Africa.

Malaria is responsible for about 450,000 deaths a year. International campaigns have significantly reduced this figure – in 2000 the number of deaths was double the present figure. Swaziland is moving to becoming the first malaria-free country in sub-Saharan Africa (the area that suffers most from the disease).

Source 2

Average wealth per adult in dollars – by region

Africa	5,080
Asia	31,715
Europe	135,977
South America	22,997
North America	340,340

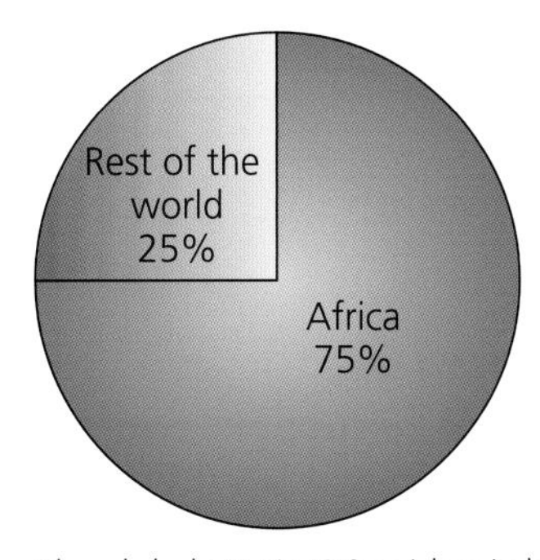

The global HIV/AIDS epidemic by percentage

Foreign aid as a percentage of gross national income (GNI)

United Kingdom	0.70
Germany	0.40
France	0.35
Canada	0.25
Japan	0.19
United States	0.19
Italy	0.16

Source 3

Estimated world deaths from malaria

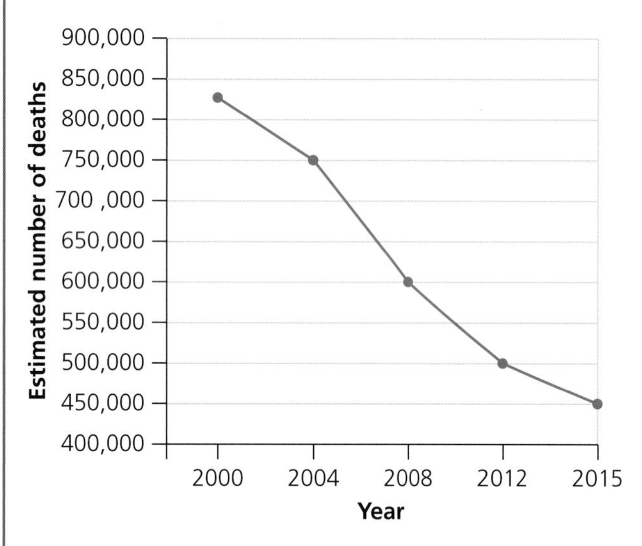

Using Sources 1, 2 and 3, what **conclusions** can be drawn about progress in development and aid?

You should reach a conclusion about each of the following:

- the progress made in reducing deaths from malaria
- the progress among rich countries to achieve the agreed GNI target on development spending
- the link between regional poverty and deaths from malaria
- the area of the world most affected by the global HIV/AIDS epidemic.

Your conclusions **must** be supported by evidence from the sources. You should link information within and between the sources in support of your conclusions.

Your answer must be based on all **three** sources. **10 marks**

Remember

- You must make an original conclusion.
- You should use more than one source to support each original conclusion.
- Use all three sources in your answer.
- For full marks, four developed conclusions must be given.

Model answer

The progress made in reducing deaths from malaria

Significant progress has been made in reducing deaths from malaria.

This is supported in Source 1 which states that the number of deaths since 2000 have been almost halved. Source 3 highlights that in 2000, over 800,000 people died from malaria. In 2015 it was 450,000. Swaziland could soon become the first country in sub-Saharan Africa to eradicate the disease.

The progress among rich countries to achieve the agreed GNI targets on development spending

Progress has been very poor with only one country achieving the agreed target.

This is supported in Source 1 which states that the wealthiest countries have failed to honour their promised increase to 0.7% of their GDI. Source 2 highlights that only the UK has reached the 0.7 % GDI target, with the USA spending a miserly figure of only 0.19%.

The link between regional poverty and deaths from malaria

The region with the lowest wealth per adult (Africa) has the highest deaths from malaria.

This is supported in Source 2 which highlights that Africa has by far the lowest regional average wealth per adult. Even the second poorest region in terms of poverty, South America, is over five times wealthier than the African figure of 500 dollars. Source 1 highlights that in 2014 an estimated 90% of those who died from malaria lived in Africa, a staggeringly high number.

The area of the world most affected by the global HIV/AIDS epidemic

The area of the world most affected by the global HIV/AIDS epidemic is Africa.

This is supported in Source 1 which highlights that the highest number of those infected live in Africa. This is supported by Source 2 which shows that a staggering three out of every four world citizens affected by HIV/AIDS live in Africa.

Marker's comment

This is an excellent answer as the candidate uses separate paragraphs for each conclusion. The candidate makes an original conclusion in each paragraph and provides evidence from two sources to support each of the four conclusions. The candidate provides detailed exemplification from the sources to further support each statement and all three sources are used.

Each of the candidate's paragraphs is worth 3 marks but as the maximum mark is 10, a full 10 marks are awarded. **10 marks**